Carl Heinrich Cornill

The Prophets of Israel

Popular Sketches from Old Testament. Third Edition

Carl Heinrich Cornill

The Prophets of Israel
Popular Sketches from Old Testament. Third Edition

ISBN/EAN: 9783744727228

Printed in Europe, USA, Canada, Australia, Japan

Cover: Foto ©Lupo / pixelio.de

More available books at **www.hansebooks.com**

THE PROPHETS OF ISRAEL

BY THE SAME AUTHOR.

THE RISE OF THE PEOPLE OF ISRAEL. A brief, popular essay in *Epitomes of Three Sciences*, also containing Prof. H. Oldenberg's "Study of Sanskrit" and Prof. J. Jastrow's "Aspects of Modern Psychology." Pages, 140. Cloth, 75 cents.

THE OPEN COURT PUBLISHING CO.
324 DEARBORN ST., CHICAGO.

THE
PROPHETS OF ISRAEL

POPULAR SKETCHES FROM

OLD TESTAMENT HISTORY

BY

CARL HEINRICH CORNILL

DOCTOR OF THEOLOGY AND PROFESSOR OF OLD TESTAMENT HISTORY
IN THE UNIVERSITY OF KÖNIGSBERG

TRANSLATED BY

SUTTON F. CORKRAN

THIRD EDITION

CHICAGO
THE OPEN COURT PUBLISHING COMPANY
(LONDON: KEGAN PAUL, TRENCH, TRUEBNER & CO.)
1897

COPYRIGHT BY
THE OPEN COURT PUBLISHING CO.
CHICAGO, ILL., 1895.

AUTHOR'S PREFACE.

NO BRANCH of science, in the last generation, has undergone such a profound revolution as that of Old Testament research. In place of the traditional representation of the religious history of Israel has been substituted a rigorous historical mode of view, which discovers in the process in question an organic development, and assigns to each event its logical position in the whole, by reference to which all the facts are severally comprehended and explained. At first, even professional scholars received this organic view of the Old Testament with repugnance and distrust; for it was no light task to abandon a position that for two thousand years had been regarded as the absolute truth. But by that power of conviction which always inheres in what is intrinsically correct, it gradually increased its dominance over men's minds, and has, particularly since the brilliant and fascinating exposition of Wellhausen's *History of Israel* of the year 1878, been borne onwards in an irresistible and uninterrupted career of triumph.

For no part of the Old Testament literature has this change of view been more significant and momentous than for the prophets, whose real significance could only now be understood and properly valued. Whilst according to the traditional view the prophets merely deepened and broadened in single points the religion of Moses, which he was supposed to have promulgated as a complete and finished system, it now appeared that the prophets had completely revolutionised the religion of Israel, that it was wholly through them that the national religion founded by Moses became a religion of the world, and that it was they who prepared and fitted the religion of Israel to become the parent of Christianity.

Truths of such importance, and so recently acquired, concerning things which affect every man's dearest interests, should not be restricted to a small band of scholars, as if constituting an esoteric doctrine; but every educated man and woman has a right to hear and to know about them. This is the purpose which this little book is designed to serve. It presupposes no special knowledge, but seeks simply to give a popular presentation of its subject-matter. It explains first the nature and import of Israelitic prophecy: indicating what in Israel's own view a prophet was; how prophecy is to be explained, and what position it occupies in the history of the religion of Israel; what its presuppositions are, and in what manner, thus, it sheds light on the period preceding it. To this is added an attempt at a historical valuation of Elijah, who occupies in so far a place apart as we possess nothing written from him. Next, the productions of the prophetic literature of Israel which have been preserved are examined in the chronological order established by Old Testament inquiry as the result of profound and laborious research. The historical conditions and the contemporary environment of the various prophets are portrayed, their significance, their peculiar original achievements briefly characterised, and finally the attempt made to assign and establish for each prophet in the developmental process of the religion of Israel his logical and organic position—in what respect his influence was promotive, and in what respect reactionary; so that the little book may be viewed as a brief sketch, giving only the salient and important outlines, of the religious history of Israel from Moses down to the time of the Maccabees.

The book grew out of a course of lectures which I was invited to deliver at the *Freie Deutsche Hochstift* in my native city of Frankfort-on-the-Main, at the request of its indefatigable director, Prof. V. Valentin. I accepted this invitation with pleasure and gratefully seized the opportunity of presenting to cultured laymen some portrayal of this grandest event in the history of religion before Christ. The idea of making a book out of my unpretentious sketch, (it does not claim to be more, and the professional scholar will recognise in it at once Wellhausen, Kuenen, Duhm, Stade, Smend, and others,) never occurred to me, and I was at first firm in my refusal to publish it. But the solicitations became finally so pressing and kind that I found it impossible not to accede to them, and overcame my hesitation. It is my hope that the printed book will have as good results as the spoken word, and accomplish its purpose of affording to persons who are deprived of access to the latest works of Old Testament science, some insight into its results and into the spirit and purpose of its inquiries. In the passages which I have literally cited from the prophetic books I have, of course, complied with the requirements of textual criticism, and I hope that my readers will not take it amiss if they are frequently found to depart from the traditional text.[1]

May, then, my unassuming pages contribute their mite towards promoting the general understanding of Israelitic prophecy, and winning for it that love and admiration which cannot fail to follow on its being understood.

C. H. CORNILL.

KÖNIGSBERG, February, 1894.

---

[1] In the English translation of the Bible passages the Old or the Revised Version has been used except where the text demanded the rendering of Professor Cornill.—*Trans.*

PUBLISHERS' PREFACE.

"Search the Scriptures."—*St. John, I'., 39.*

THE Bible is unqualifiedly that collection of books in the literature of mankind which has exercised the most potent influence over the civilisation of the world. Yet it is little read, and where it is read it is much misunderstood. The pious exalt it as the word of God, and believe in its very letter, as best they can; while infidels point out its incongruities and pillory its monstrosities. Need we add that only the mistaken pretensions of the former justify the caustic sarcasm of the latter?

If we read the Bible, not with an open mind, but devoutly, with a complete submission of judgment, we are as apt to distort its meaning, and render ourselves unfit to comprehend its purport, as is the iconoclast, who goes over its pages with no other intention than to seek out absurdities.

There is, however, another attitude which we can take towards the Bible. It is that of a reader impartial in investigation and eager to learn.

He who studies the Bible, not as a partisan, but as a scholar, in the same spirit that the historian studies Greek and Roman literature, finds the Biblical books invaluable, for they are the precious documents of the religious evolution of mankind. Such men as Goethe, Humboldt, and Huxley, the great pagans of modern times, had only words of praise for the Bible; they found in it an inexhaustible source of wisdom and poetry.

The work of earnest study, comparison, and investigation has been undertaken by a number of intrepid scholars, who have devoted their lives to the interpretation of the Scriptures. The foundation was laid by what is commonly called "text-critique," or "the Lower Criticism," which implies a collation of the various manuscripts, a restoration of doubtful readings, and the determination of exact definitions of words or phrases. This done, "the Higher Criticism" can attack the more important problems of the origin of a book, its place in history, its significance, and the purpose which the author had in view in writing it.

It is a matter of course that the methods of the Higher Criticism alone enable us to understand and appreciate the Bible. Nevertheless earnest believers are full of anxiety on account of the negative results of scientific Bible-research, which, in their opinion, threatens to destroy Christianity, and appears to leave nothing tangible to believe in or to hope for. The Higher Criticism appears alarming to the old orthodoxy, for nothing seems left which can be relied upon.

Orthodoxy means "right doctrine," and it is but natural to think that if the old conception of orthodoxy has become untenable, scepticism will prevail, and that we must be satisfied with the resigned position of agnosticism, proclaiming that nothing can be known for certain. But because the old conception of orthodoxy fails, there is no reason to say that orthodoxy itself, in the original and proper sense of the term, is a vain hope. Bear in mind that the endeavor to establish an unquestionable orthodoxy on the solid foundation of evidence is founded in the very nature of science.

The negations of the Biblical criticism are only a preliminary work, which prepares the way for positive issues. Scepticism may be a phase through which we have to pass, but it is not the end. The final result will be the recognition of a new and a higher orthodoxy—the orthodoxy of provable truth, which discards the belief in the letter, but preserves the spirit, and stands in every respect as high above the old orthodoxy as astronomy ranks above astrology.

Prof. Carl Heinrich Cornill is an orthodox Christian. He holds the chair of Old Testament history in the venerable University of Königsberg. But, being a Christian and at the same time a scientific man, he has devoted his life to the investigation of the religious evolution of the Israelitic and Christian faiths. Thus he serves both Christ and Science.

Is not this position inconsistent? Does it not involve that a critic serves two masters? Let us see.

What shall a Christian scholar do if the injunctions of Christ come into conflict with science? First he may doubt the exactness of the scientific argument, and keep his judgment suspended until better evidence is forthcoming. But suppose the evidence comes and the conflict still remains? Exactly in anticipation of such possibilities the opinion is often set up that it is wrong for a Christian to subject the documents of his faith to a scientific critique, and he is requested to accept them blindly without inquiry.

We venture to differ, and would say, as it is a man's duty to investigate nature and to invent machinery for the sake of his bodily prosperity, so it is the more his duty to inquire into the central problem of life, which is religion, so that he may the better learn to take care of his soul. Investigation is a religious duty. In this sense Christ says: "Search the Scriptures; for in them ye think ye have eternal life; and they are they which testify of me."

Christ himself requests us to search, and should the results of our search really come into conflict with Christ's injunctions, must we not assume that there is something wrong either in our science or in our conception of Christ? Instead of giving up all investigation for this reason, we must, on the contrary, continue to search until we find both Christ and Science in perfect agreement.

But there is danger in superficiality! Some take a few apparently obvious but one-sided observations as the final verdict of science, while others worship a Christ who is merely a pagan idol that has received a Christian finish.

Science is often regarded as a human invention in which sense it is considered as profane and contrasted to the truth of God. But is Science really a human invention? Can man fashion Science as he pleases? Is it an expression of his subjectivism? Can its propositions be suited to our likes and dislikes? Certainly not! On the contrary, Science is a revelation of truth, and its nature is stern and unalterable objectivity. Science is superhuman, and scientific truth partakes of that eternity which is predicated of God; for, indeed the truth is of God. If Science is truly Science, it is God's revelation, and he who is afraid of a conflict between Religion and Science, must be on his guard lest his Religion, though dear to him, be a mere superstition. A Religion that comes into conflict with Science is doomed, be it ever so pleasing to the human heart. Religion must always remain in accord with Science, for Science is not profane; Science is holy. If God ever spoke to man, Science is the fiery bush. Science is a religious revelation.

Professor Cornill, in speaking of the scientist's freedom of investigation, says:

"Am I not speaking in behalf of the most boundless and devotionless subjectivism? Indeed not. I demand complete freedom only for *scientific* criticism, and that carries within itself its own corrective. Science is a sovereign power, which proceeds in accordance with rules of its own, yet is unconditionally bound to law: *without law, without discipline, no true science is conceivable.* But to that which has been acquired through strict and methodical scientific research, we are bound to bow unconditionally, be it welcome to us or not; confidently trusting that, like every good gift, so also science is not a work of the Devil, but comes from God."

We seek for catholicity in Religion, and lo, we have it in Science, for we may define Science as that upon which all those who thoroughly understand a problem must finally agree. Science digs down to the bed-rock of truth and if anything can reveal to us the bed-rock of ages upon which our religious faith rests, it is Science.

We do not mean to say that Science is sufficient, but we do say that Science is indispensable. Mere intellectual comprehension, it is true, has no saving power; it is without avail if the emotional side of man's soul remains neglected, (for the heart is after all the mainspring of our actions.) But the heart, if not illumined by the head, is like a man groping in the dark. Disregard of Science leads men astray, and we do not hesitate to brand a contempt of Science as a religious fault, as a sin. It is not based upon strength of faith, but indicates a lack of Faith, and, indeed, it is the expression of the highest impertinence and arrogance a man is capable of, that of raising his opinion, his private belief of what the Truth ought to be, against actual Truth, the Truth as it is revealed to the world.

Genuine Religion will always encourage Science. We must investigate and acquire knowledge, we must exercise critique, and we must respect the authority of scientific demonstration. But our knowledge must become conviction, and conviction, if it becomes the motive power of a moral life, is called Faith. There is no merit in belief. A blind acceptance of religious traditions is not recommendable; but Faith, that is, a living conviction well founded upon a basis which we know to be the Truth, is the ultimate aim of Religion.

PAUL CARUS,
Manager of The Open Court Publishing Co.

P. S.—As it was impossible to send proofs of this book to Mr. Sutton F. Corkran, who lives in Europe, Mr. Thomas J. McCormack has carefully revised the translation and collated the manuscript with the original, and he is responsible for its final form.

TABLE OF CONTENTS.

	PAGE
The Meaning of Prophecy	1
The Religion of Moses	16
The Early Prophets.—Elijah.—Elisha	27
Amos	37
Hosea	47
Isaiah.—Micah	57
The Reaction Against the Prophets.—Micah (Chaps. 6–7).—Zephaniah.—Nahum.—Habakkuk	71
Deuteronomy	80
Jeremiah	91
The Babylonian Exile	108
Ezekiel	115
The Literary Achievements of the Exile	125
Deutero-Isaiah	131
The Return from the Captivity.—Haggai.—Zechariah	145
Ezra and Nehemiah.—Malachi	155
The Later Prophets.—Joel.—Obadiah.—Isaiah (Chaps. 24–27).—Zechariah (Chaps. 9–14)	164
Jonah and Daniel.—The Maccabees.—Conclusion	170

THE MEANING OF PROPHECY.

THERE is none of us but knows of the existence of the prophets of the Old Testament, having learnt in the Sabbath-school the outlandish names of those sixteen men, and on account of their very unwontedness perhaps retained them in the memory. Possibly, also, some one or other of the so-called apophthegms from their writings have remained familiar to us. But here our acquaintance ceases. Who those men were, what they aspired for and did, what they were for their time, and what they still are for us, the average educated person of to-day may have some dim inkling, but in no wise a correct or clear idea. Nor is this to be wondered at. Neither can any one be blamed for it. If, in general, the books of the Old Testament are not easily understood by the laity, this is especially true as regards the prophetic books. They are in the veriest sense "books with seven seals." Does not Isaiah himself in a very remarkable passage compare prophecy to a sealed book, of which the mere perusal does not suffice. Not that the prophets wrote in an especially obscure or abstruse style. The difficulty of understanding them is not of the kind that confronts us when reading Dante's *Divina Comedia*, or the second part of *Faust*, though such instances do occur in the prophetic literature, as, for example, in the visions of the book of Zechariah. No, the interpretation of the mere words of the prophetic writings is mostly simple; but in perusing them the reader has a two-fold sensation: either what is said appears to him as self-evident, as being nothing wonderful or important, or it is quite unintelligible to him, because he does not know what the prophet is striving after, what he alludes to, nor what are the circumstances and situations he may be considering. Both these impressions are justified and well-founded.

The Israelitish prophecy is a distinctly historical event, and for understanding it a thorough and precise knowledge of the religious and profane history of the Jews is absolutely necessary: a thorough and precise knowledge of the religious history, so as to enable us to judge what that which appears to us self-evident meant in the mouth and at the time of the man who first spoke it; and a precise and thorough knowledge of the profane history of the Israelites, so as to understand the relations under which and in which the prophets acted, and towards which their efforts were directed. It is no easy matter to obtain such a thorough and complete command of the religious and secular history of the Israelites. This goal is to be reached only by much labor and on circuitous paths, for the Israelitish narrative, as it lies before us in the books of the Old Testament, gives a thoroughly one-sided and in many respects incorrect picture of the profane history, and on the other hand an absolutely false representation of the religious history of the people, and has thus made the discovery of the truth well-nigh impossible.

At the time when the historical books of the Old Testament were put into the final form in which they now lie before us, during and after the Babylonian exile, the past was no longer understood. Men were ashamed of it. They could not understand that in the days of old all had been so completely different, and therefore did all in their power to erase and blot out in their accounts of the past whatever at this later date might be a cause of offence.

In the same manner the Arabs, after their conversion to Islam, purposely obliterated all traces of the era of "folly," as they term the pre-Islamitic period of their existence, so that it gives one the greatest difficulty to get in any wise a clear picture of the early Arabic paganism. The history of the German nation has also an analogous spectacle to show in the blind and ill-advised zeal of the Christian converts who systematically destroyed the old pagan literature, which a man like Charles the Great had gathered together with such love and appreciation. This, luckily, the men to whom we owe the compilation and final redaction of the ancient Israelitish literature did not do; they were satisfied with emendations and corrections, and left enough standing to afford, at least to the trained eye of the modern critic, a sufficient groundwork for unravelling the truth.

The newest phase of Old Testament investigation has succeeded in raising this veil, now more than two thousand years old, and through an act similar to that of Copernicus, by which, so to speak, the narrative was turned upside down, has brought out the real historical truth. I can assert without any personal presumption, as I am only a worker and not a discoverer in this particular field, that a thorough comprehension of the Israelitish prophecy has only been possible within the last twenty-five years, as it is only since this date that the true course and the real development of the Israelitish religious history has been ascertained, and because also the discovery and deciphering of the cuneiform inscriptions have given us a more thorough understanding of the secular history of ancient Israel. I may hope, therefore, in the remarks which are to follow and to which I now ask your attention, to be able to offer something new to such of my hearers as have not followed the latest developments of Old Testament research.

But before we enter upon our study of the Israelitish prophecy, we must first answer the question, "What is a prophet?" It will be seen that the very definition of the term is beset with difficulties and miscomprehenions.

We all use the word "prophet," and have some sort of idea of what we mean. But if we should be asked what we meant, our answer would probably be: "That is clear and intelligible enough. A prophet is a man who predicts the future. This is plainly indicated in the name: πρό means 'before,' and φημί 'I say'; hence, προφήτης, prophet, means a foreteller." And this will apparently be confirmed by the subject, for all the so-called prophets of the Old Testament busied themselves with the future, and according to the popular view their special duty and importance consists in having foretold the coming of Christ. But, however widespread this view may be and however generally the interpretation be accepted, it is nevertheless incorrect, and in no wise just to the character and to the importance of the Israelitish prophecy. That this can never have been the original conception of the Israelites, may be thoroughly proved by an irrefutable etymological argument. The Semitic languages generally do not possess the power of forming compound words; consequently, the idea of foretelling cannot be expressed in them by a simple word. Even the Greek word προφήτης, in spite of its obvious etymology, does not possess this meaning; the men who foresee and foretell the future the Greek calls μάντις; to call Kalchas, or Teiresias, *prophetes* would have been wrong in Greek.

If we wish to gain a clear understanding of the Israelitish prophecy, we must first of all determine what the Israelites themselves understood by a prophet. We find nowhere in the Old Testament a clear definition of the term; we must seek, accordingly, to arrive at its interpretation by another way. And that way is the etymological. In no language are words originally mere empty sounds, conventional formulæ; they are always proper names. Man seizes upon some salient feature, some characteristic property of the thing to be defined, and names and defines the thing according to that property. Thus the science of language grants us an insight into periods and times far back of all historical tradition, and we can, on the basis of the science of language, reconstruct the history of civilisation and the ethics of the remotest periods; for the names of a language are, so to speak, the precipitates of the civilisation and moral views of the people inventing them.

When the common word for father in all the Indo-Germanic languages denotes the supporter and breadwinner, it is to be clearly seen from this fact that the old Aryans looked upon fatherhood not merely as a natural relationship, but as a moral duty, that to them the father was not in the first place a begetter, but also the food-giver, the supporter, the protector and provider of his family, that the original heads of families of the Indo-Europeans were not rude savages, but men of deep ethical feelings, who had already higher moral perceptions than the average man of the present day. And when our word *daughter* (*Tochter*), which can be traced through a number of Indo-Germanic languages, and therefore belongs to the general Indo-Germanic primitive stock, means in reality the *milker*, we may again draw from this, very important conclusions respecting the civilisation of those early times: we may conclude that the heads of the Indo-Germanic tribes were engaged in raising cattle, and that all the work was carried on by the family itself, that the institution of slavery was entirely foreign to them, for which we have the further positive proof that the Indo-Germanic languages possess no word in common for this idea, that it did not yet exist when they separated from one another. And now, to take two examples from the Semitic group of languages which is immediately occupying our attention, when the common Semitic word for king, *melek*, denotes, according to the root-meaning still preserved in the Aramaic, the "counsellor"; when the common Semitic word for God, *êl*, denotes etymologically the "goal," that is, him or that to which all human longing aspires and must aspire; when, therefore, by this word for God religion is defined by the early Semites as a problem for man with a promise of its final solution, it follows with irrefutable clearness that the much defamed and much despised Semites, are in no wise such an inferior race, or such worthless men, as it is unfortunately at the present day the fashion to depict them.

After this short digression now, let us turn our attention to the attempt to explain the ancient Israelitish notions of the character of a prophet by etymology. Here, however, we must point out the very important fact, that with the original etymological sense, the real meaning of the word at the time we actually meet it, is very far from determined, for both language and individuals words have their history. Thus, the word *marshal* means etymologically a "groom" or "hostler," yet at the present day we understand by this word something quite different from a groom. It is the very task, in fact, of the history of language and of civilisation to show how the actual traditional meaning has been developed from the primitive etymological signification.

The Hebrew language calls the prophet *nābi*. It immediately strikes us, that this word has as little an obvious Hebrew etymology as the word *kôhēn* (priest) or as the specifically Israelitic name of God, which we are in the habit of pronouncing Jehovah. Now, if we are unable to explain the word *nābi* satisfactorily from the Hebrew, a most important conclusion follows: the word cannot be specifically Israelitish, but must have been transplanted to Israel before the historical period. We must therefore turn to the other Semitic languages for information, and must assume that the home of the word in question is to be sought for in that branch of the Semitic group where the etymology is still plain and lucid. We still meet with the root *naba'a* in the

Assyrian-Babylonian and in the Arabic. In Assyrian it simply means "to speak," "to talk," "to announce," "to name," the substantive derived from it meaning "announcement," "designation"; from it comes also the name of the well-known Babylonian god *Nebo*, Babylonian *Nabu*, which is to be found as the first part of a large number of Babylonian names, such as Nabopolassar and Nebuchadnezzar; whilst it also follows from the original root that this Babylonian god Nabu, is the god of wisdom, of science, of the word, and of speech, whom the Greeks identified with Hermes, and after whom to the present day the planet Mercury is named.

Considered by the light of this Assyrian-Babylonian etymology the Hebraic *nābī* would have the meaning of speaker, and ordinarily that would satisfy us; for in former days the efficacy of a prophet was entirely personal and oral. But every orator is not a preacher, and not every one who speaks, a prophet; therefore in this Assyrian-Babylonian etymology the most important point is lacking, namely, all indication of the characteristic quality of the prophetic speech. We obtain this through the Arabic. The primitive Semitic type has been preserved most purely in the Arabic, and the Arabic language has therefore for the scientific investigation of the Semitic languages the same importance as Sanskrit has for the Indo-Germanic, and, indeed, a much higher one, for Arabic is more closely related to the primitive Semitic than is Sanskrit to the primitive Indo-Germanic. Now, the Arabic has also the root *naba'a*, but never in the general sense of "speaking," as in the Assyrian-Babylonian, but in the thoroughly special sense of "proclaiming," "announcing," *naba'a* or *anba'a* being he who proclaims something definite, or has to carry out some mandate. The specific significance lies therefore in the Arabic root, that this speaker discourses not of himself, nor of anything special to himself, but on some distinctive instigation, or as agent for some other person; according to this the *nābī* would be the *deputed* speaker, he who has to declare some special communication, who has to deliver some message, and here we have lighted upon the real essence and pith of the matter.

That a trace of this fundamental signification has been preserved in the Hebrew, can be proved from a very characteristic passage in Exodus. Moses has declined the charge to appear before Pharaoh, saying: "I am not eloquent . . . but I am slow of speech and of a slow tongue." And then God says to him that his brother Aaron can speak well, he shall be his spokesman, and this is thus expressed: "Behold, I have made thee a god to Pharaoh, and Aaron, thy brother, shall be thy prophet: thou shalt speak all that I command thee, and Aaron, thy brother, shall speak unto Pharaoh." Thus Aaron is prophet to Moses, because he speaks for him; he is his spokesman. Who it is that gives the charge and speaks in the prophet, so called, is not far to seek: it is God. And with this meaning the technical sense of the Greek word προ-φήτης agrees in the most wonderful manner. According to the Greeks the προφήτης is he who interprets and translates into clear, intelligible language the incomprehensible oracles of the gods: at Dodona, the rustling of the sacred oak of Zeus; at Delphi, the inarticulate utterances and ecstatic cries of the Pythia. In the same sense, also, Pindar can describe himself as a prophet of the muse, because he speaks only what the muse inspires in him. Thus, in the Hebrew *nābî* we have him who speaks not of himself, but according to higher command, in the name and as the messenger of God to Israel; in the Greek προφήτης, him who transmits and explains to those around him the oracles of the gods.

Thus is the conception of the prophet, as he appears to us in the Israelitish books, thoroughly explained. All these men have the consciousness of not acting in their own personal capacities, of not pronouncing the sentiments of their own minds, but as the instruments of a Higher Being, who acts and speaks through them; they feel themselves to be, as Jeremiah expresses it once in a remarkably characteristic verse, "the mouth of God."

As the Arabic language gives us the only satisfactory explanation of the word, we must suppose Arabia to be the home of prophecy, and as a fact the visionary and ecstatic elements which attach to prophesying, and which the Israelitish prophecies alone overcame and cast off, savor somewhat of the desert. The first great prophet of whom we find an account in the Old Testament, Elijah, was not a native of Palestine proper, but came from the country east of Jordan, the boundary-land, where it has been proved that a strong mixture of Arabic blood took place. Besides, the other neighboring tribes had also their prophets. In the history of Elijah we meet with the Phœnician prophets of Baal, and Jeremiah also speaks of prophets in all surrounding countries.

That the word *nābī* has in fact had a history, and that prophesying was looked upon originally as something extraneous, is distinctly testified to us in a very remarkable passage. If we glance over the history of Israel, the prophet Samuel, after Moses, appears as the most important personage. Now Samuel, in the oldest records we have concerning him, is never called prophet, but always "seer," and some later hand has added the invaluable explanatory remark that that which then was called prophet, was called in olden times in Israel "seer."

What was understood in those older days by prophet, we learn from the same narrative, where it is announced to Saul as a sign: That "it shall come to pass that when thou art come thither to the city, that thou shalt meet a company of prophets coming down from the high place with a psaltery and a tabret and a pipe and a harp before them, and they shall prophesy: And the spirit of the Lord shall come upon thee, and thou shalt prophesy with them." And as it came to pass all the people of Gibea asked in astonishment, "Is Saul also among the prophets?" which does not mean: "How is it that such a worldly-minded man finds himself in the company of such pious people?" but is to be interpreted as meaning: "How comes a person of such distinction to find himself in such low company?" In these prophets of the time of Saul, where we first meet them, we have the type of the original form which prophesying assumed on Canaanite soil; they are men after the manner of Mohammedan fakirs, or dancing and howling dervishes, who express their religious exaltation through their eccentric mode of life, and thus it comes that the Hebrew word *hithnabbē*, which means "to live as a prophet," has also the signification "to rave, to behave in an unseemly manner."

The genuine counterpart of these ecstatic fakirs may be found in the priests of Baal at the time of Elijah, who danced round the altar of Baal shouting and cutting themselves with knives, in order to produce an impression on their god. Such prophets lived together in Israel until a very late date in guilds, the so-called schools of the prophets. They wore a coarse, hairy cloak as the garb of their order, and existed on charity, a species of begging-friars, and evidently were not regarded with great respect. To Ahab they prophesied whatsoever was pleasing to him to hear, and as one of them came into the camp unto Jehu with a message from Elisha to anoint him king, his friends asked him "wherefore came this mad fellow to thee?" Amos likewise resents being placed on the same level with these begging prophets, "I was no prophet, neither was I a prophet's son: but I was an herdman and a gatherer of sycomore fruit."

Rudiments of this originally ecstatic type are found even among the great prophets, as when it is recorded of Elijah that he outran the king's chariot going at full speed on the road from Karmel to Jezreel, or when Elisha caused a harper to play, in order to arouse by music the prophetic inspiration. Even among the prophets whose writings have come down to us we find isolated traces of violence and eccentricity.

If we compare, however, a Hosea or a Jeremiah with these savage dervishes, the examination of prophetism will yield the same result which we observe everywhere, that all that Israel borrowed from others it so regenerated and stamped with its own identity, that it becomes difficult to recognise in the beauteous Israelitish creation and transformation any trace of the original. For this reason one should not be loath to recognise the many foreign elements in the religion of Israel; in doing so we do not lower it, but quite the contrary, we bear witness to its tremendous vital power and invincible capacity for assimilation. Israel resembles in spiritual things the fabulous king Midas who turned everything he touched into gold.

But to appreciate the position which prophetism assumes in the development of the Israelitish religion and to be able to understand how in Israel this thorough transformation of prophesying could be effected, we must attempt to render clear to ourselves the course of evolution of the Israelitish religion.

THE RELIGION OF MOSES.

I MUST preface my remarks with the statement, which is to-day not superfluous, that I regard the traditions of Israel concerning its ancient history on the whole as historical. They are to be accepted with reserve and criticism, as all legends are, but at the basis of them is to be found a grain of historical truth, which it is the duty of the historian to disengage from the magic veil which legend has woven round it. I believe, accordingly, that the forefathers of Israel under the guidance of Abraham wandered from Haran in Mesopotamia into Palestine; that after a long sojourn there and after many adventures they wended their way into Egypt and settled down in the pasture-lands of the Eastern Nile-delta; that they met there at first with a friendly reception, or at least were tolerated, but at last were heavily oppressed, till under the guidance of Moses, who belonged to the tribe of Levi, but who through a special concatenation of circumstances had received access to the higher civilisation and culture of Egypt, they succeeded in freeing themselves from the Egyptian yoke. The entire Hebraic tradition with one accord regards this Moses, the leader of the exodus out of Egypt, as the founder of the religion of Israel. Our first question, therefore, must be : What sort of religion was this that Moses founded? In what did its novelty consist?

And now I must make an admission to you, which it is hard for me to make, but which is my fullest scientific conviction, based upon the most cogent grounds, that in the sense in which the historian speaks of "knowing," we know absolutely nothing about Moses. All original records are missing; we have not received a line, not even a word, from Moses himself, or from any of his contemporaries; even the celebrated Ten Commandments are not from him, but, as can be proved, were written in the first half of the seventh century between 700 and 650 B.C. The oldest accounts we have of Moses are five hundred years later than his time. Nevertheless, this comparatively modern tradition contains some special features which are important and require to be considered in the solution of the question now occupying our attention.

They are as follows. The work of Moses does in no way appear as something absolutely new, but as a supplement to something already existing among the people. It is the "God of our fathers" that Moses proclaims. Likewise, it is certain, that the name of this God, whom we are wont to call Jehovah, and whose real Hebrew pronunciation is *Yahveh*, was first introduced by Moses, and that a priest from Sinai, whom tradition makes the father-in-law of Moses, had no mean share in Moses's work.

As regards the first of these points, all the internal evidence is in its favor. The relations and circumstances of the time were not suited to an entirely new creation; had the people at the time of Moses been common Semitic heathens or Egyptian animal-worshippers, his achievements would have been unintelligible. Moreover, I believe we can bring into organic connexion with this theory one of the most charming and touching narratives in Genesis, the narrative of how Abraham originally intended to sacrifice his only son, Isaac, to God as a burnt-offering, when an angel appeared and placed in his stead a ram. (Among the Canaanites the sacrifice of children was an ancient and holy institution.) The only purpose the narrative can have is to show how Abraham and his companions in their wholesome and unpolluted minds regarded this institution with horror, and that they kept themselves uncontaminated by the religious customs of the Canaanites among whom they lived, and whose language they adopted. To ascertain and establish the belief of Abraham is an utterly impossible task, but that Israel possessed before the time of Moses some definite type of religion, on which Moses could build, is a conclusion from which we cannot escape.

The two other points distinctly traceable in the Hebrew tradition regarding Moses, namely, that the name of God "Yahveh" was first introduced into Israel by him, and that a religious relationship existed with Sinai, where tradition places the foundation of the Israelitic religion by Moses, are also confirmed by closer examination and found to be connected.

In the first place, we are struck with the fact that the name of God "Yahveh" has no obvious Hebrew etymology. The interpretation of this word was a matter of difficulty and uncertainty even for the Old Testament itself. In Hebrew, the verb "to be" alone could come into consideration. This in the Hebrew is *hajdh*, but in Aramaic *hewd*, with a *w* in the second place. We must, however, ask: Why did Moses, if he himself invented the name, derive it, not from the Hebrew, but from the Aramaic, form of the verb "to be," whilst we cannot prove, or even render probable, the least connexion or influence on the part of the Aramaic language? And, moreover, this derivation is in itself in the highest degree suspicious and doubtful. A name for God, that expressed nothing more of God than mere being, essence, pure existence, is hard to conceive of at such an ancient period; all this is the pale cast of philosophical speculation, but not the virile life of religion, and with such a purely speculative name of God, Moses would have given to his people a stone instead of bread. Feeling this difficulty the attempt has been made to derive the name from the causative form, which in Semitic is obtained by a simple vowel-change in the radical, as we form *set* from *sit*, *fell* from *fall*; in which case we should have to render "Yahveh," not as "He that is" but as "He that calls into existence." But no Hebrew, and no Semite, of those days, ever described the creative power of God as a "calling into existence"; a causative form of the verb "to be" is nowhere found in all the Semitic tongues.

Here again, as with the word *nābî*, prophet, the Arabic helps us out of our difficulties. The Arabic has still preserved the fundamental meaning of this root: *hawā* means "to fall," and of this meaning the root in Hebrew has still retained at least one distinct trace; the idea of "falling" is connected with "to be" by the intermediary conception, "to fall out," "to occur." Now observe the following facts. In olden times Sinai seems to have been looked upon as the special habitation of the God of Israel. In the oldest production of the Hebrew literature that we have, the glorious song of Deborah, God comes down from Sinai, to bring help unto his people, who are engaged in a severe struggle at Kishon with the Canaanites; and the prophet Elijah made a pilgrimage unto Horeb, as Sinai is known under another name, to seek the Lord in person. The Arabic, thus, gives us a concrete explanation of the name "Yahveh": it would mean "the feller," the god of the storms, who by his thunderbolts fells and lays low his enemies.

That Yahveh was originally a god of tempests may be shown by many additional vestiges, and this was distinctly recognised at a time when no one thought of thus explaining the name. When He first shows Himself to Moses and to the people on Sinai, He appears in the midst of a terrible storm, and in the poetry of Israel it is also customary to depict the theophanies as storms. In the cherubs on which He rides, one skilled in the interpretation of mythological ideas sees at once a personification of the storm-clouds; and the seraphs, which, however, are mentioned only by Isaiah, are obviously a personification of the serpent of heaven, of the lightning.

And now I should like to call your attention to another very important fact. This strange form of the name of God, Yahveh, which is a verbal form, an imperfect, finds, in the whole populous Pantheon of the heathen Semites, analogies only on Arabian soil: among the hundreds of Semitic names of God known to us, we can point to but four such formations, and all of them occur on Arabian soil. The Sinai peninsula belongs linguistically and ethnographically to Arabia, and when we keep all these facts before us, the conviction is forced upon us that Yahveh was originally the name of one of the gods worshipped on Mount Sinai, which from the earliest times was considered holy, and that Moses adopted this name, and bestowed it on the God of Israel, the God of their fathers.

But now you will ask, with some astonishment, is this, then, really all that we can infer about Moses, even granting we *know* nothing about him? No, it is not. But, to learn more, we must employ a somewhat more circuitous method. Even that most exact of all sciences, mathematics, regards a so-called indirect proof as equally convincing with a direct one, if it be rightly worked out, and such an indirect proof we possess for determining the work of Moses. We may employ, in fact, the method of inference from effect to cause. Since, according to the universally accepted tradition of the whole people of Israel, Moses is the founder of the specifically Israelitic religion, we have only to establish what this was, and in doing so we establish at the same time the work of Moses.

To this end, we must first seek to discover the constituent elements of the religious consciousness of Israel as it existed in the minds of the people before the prophets gave to it wholly new impulses. We have, moreover, to compare this religious belief of the people of Israel about the year 800 B.C. with the religious ideas which we find elsewhere in the Semitic races, and with the conceptions of those purely or not purely Semitic races, with whom Israel came into direct contact, as the Egyptians and the Babylonians. What we find by such a comparison to agree completely with the conceptions of the other Semitic tribes, can in Israel also be a spontaneous production of the Semitic mind, just as in the other Semitic tribes; while that finally which corresponds with the conceptions of the Babylonians or Egyptians, can have been borrowed directly from them, because the conditions of such an origin exist in the long sojourn of the Israelites among those nations. Should, however, in the religion of Israel, about 800 B. C., things be found, which none of the nations mentioned have in common with Israel, or such as are diametrically opposed to the conceptions and notions of those nations, then we have in such things, according to all the rules of historical and religio-scientific reasoning, a creation of Moses.

Now, as a fact, the religion of Israel exhibits a large number of such features. Israel is the only nation we know of that never had a mythology, the only people who never differentiated the Deity sexually. So deep does this last trait extend, that the Hebrew language is not even competent to form the word "goddess." Where the Book of Kings tells us of the supposed worship of idols by Solomon, we find written: "Astarte, the *god* of the Phœnicians." Not even the *word* "goddess" is conceivable to the Israelites, much less the thing itself. Similarly, the cult of Israel is distinguished by great simplicity and purity, as may be proved by such old and thoroughly Israelitic feasts as the Passover, the offering of the firstlings of the flock during the vernal equinox, and the New Moons. Israel denounces with abhorrence the sacrificing of children, and especially that religious immorality, which held full sway among the immediate neighbors of Israel, that most detestable of all religious aberrations, which considered prostitution as an act of worship. In fact,

Israel, even in its earliest days, possessed in comparison with the neighboring tribes, a very high and pure morality. For sins of unchastity the ancient Hebrew has an extremely characteristic expression: it calls them *nebaldh*, "madness," something inconceivable, unintelligible, which a reasonable and normally organised man could never commit.

But the most important feature of all is the manner in which Israel conceives its relations to God. Monotheism, in a strictly scientific sense, ancient Israel had not; Yahveh was not the only existing God in heaven and on earth; He was only the exclusive God of Israel. Israel had henotheism, as Max Müller has termed this idea to distinguish it from monotheism, and monolatry only. The Israelite could only serve Yahveh; to serve another god was for the Israelite a crime deserving of death. Thus was the relation of the Israelites to this their only God especially close and intimate; the religious instinct concentrated itself on one object, and thereby received an intensity, which is foreign to polytheism, and must ever remain foreign to it. And this one and only God of Israel was not a metaphysical entity, floating about in the grey misty regions beyond the clouds, but He was a personality, He was everywhere, and present in all things. The ways both of nature and of daily life were God's work.

And this brings us to an extremely important point. No distinction was known between divine and human law; both were God's institutions and commands, civil as well as church law, to express ourselves in more modern terms. That any valid law might be merely of human formulation and of human discovery, is for the ancient Israelite utterly inconceivable; therefore, every one that sins against the civil law sins against God—ancient Israel knew only sins, and no crimes.

Moses also understood how to make God accessible in practical life. The old priestly oracle of the Israelites, which played so important a part in the ancient days, must also be regarded as a Mosaic institution. And practically this is of the utmost importance; for by it the approach to God at every moment was made easy, and all of life was passed in the service and under the supervision of Yahveh. This is indeed much and great. Yahveh, alone the God of Israel, who suffers no one and nothing beside Him, who will belong entirely and exclusively to this people, but will also have this people belong entirely and exclusively to Him, so that it shall be a pure and pious people, whose whole life, even in the apparently most public and worldly matters, is a service of God, and this God source and shield of all justice and all morality—these must have all been the genuine and specific thoughts of Moses. Moreover, the importance of these thoughts reaches far beyond the province of religion in the narrower sense of the word. By giving to Israel a national Deity, Moses made of it a nation, and cemented together by this ideal band the different heterogeneous elements of the nation into a unity. Moses formed Israel into a people. (With Moses and his work begins the history of the people of Israel.)

This work was soon to be put to the test. About a generation after the death of Moses, Israel forced its way into Palestine and found itself before a terrible danger. The Canaanites were far superior in civilisation to the primitive sons of the desert. Israel adopted this civilisation, and passed in Canaan from the nomadic mode of life to the agricultural, finally taking up a permanent residence there. (It even took from Canaan the outward forms of religion, and in a measure adopted its holy places. The Sabbath, which the ancient Babylonians had, and which was designated as a "day of recreation for the heart," and the three great yearly festivals of the Passover, of the Weeks, and of the Tabernacles, are borrowed from the Canaanites; while the holy places of worship, Bethel, Dan, Gilgal, Beersheba, Sichem and Gibeon, Shiloh and Ramah, and others are all adopted outright from the Canaanites. But if Israel preserved its identity during this mighty process of transformation, was not spiritually overcome and conquered by the Canaanites, but, on the contrary, knew how to absorb the Canaanites themselves, so that in the end Israel remained the decisive and dominant factor, it owes this solely to Moses and his work, which gave to the Israelite nation its religious consecration and religious foundation, and made it competent, not only to preserve itself, but also to expand and to make extensive conquests.

THE EARLY PROPHETS.

AFTER this long digression on the religious and profane history of Israel, let us return to our starting-point. We see everywhere that the first impulses in all the crises of the history of Israel spring from its religion. This, the oldest production of Hebrew literature that we have, the glorious song of Deborah, shows us. (The narrative subsequently attached to this production calls Deborah a prophetess.) She was a divinely inspired woman, who in a sad and critical period knew how to infuse into her dejected countrymen a fresh confidence in God and in themselves. There scarcely exists a more eloquent testimony of this stalwart and ingenuous belief in God, and of this primitive triumphant piety than that which the song of Deborah offers. The struggle for their heavily oppressed nationality is a struggle for God, and He fights from heaven for His people ; the stars in their courses fought against Sisera and the kings of Canaan.

Similarly, at the head of the kingdom, stands Samuel, a seer enlightened of God, who bears in his prayerful heart the misery of his people, and who clearly perceives the way out of their distress and oppression, who recognises in Saul of the tribe of Benjamin the man of the time, who lights in his heroic soul the kindling spark, and gives to him the religious consecration that supports him on his way. This is all that the oldest record tells us of Samuel; a later period magnified and raised his image at the expense of Saul, upon whom falls thus the unmerited lot of being numbered among the biblical miscreants. In the oldest chronicles Saul appears as a noble hero and a pious king, over whom hangs a gloomy fate, and who finally perishes in a tragic manner.

The frequent assertion of a reforming and organising efficacy of Samuel in the province of prophesying, and that Samuel founded and was the head of the schools of prophets, is a legend of a later period which cannot stand before a methodical historical criticism.

We meet with prophets also during the reign of David. Nathan especially is known, who holds up to the king, with an invincible love of truth, his grievous sin; and a prophet Gad is also mentioned in the time of David. When Solomon by his despotic government and passion for splendor estranged himself from the hearts of Israel, we are told of a prophet Ahijah of Shiloh who encouraged Jeroboam to rebel against Solomon: "Behold, I will rend the kingdom out of the hand of Solomon and will give ten tribes to thee." Still all these men are only figures appearing in the episodes, of whom we know too little, to obtain any clear idea of their importance and efficacy.

The first prophet of Israel on a grand scale was — Elijah, one of the most titanic personages in all the Old Testament. One has at once the impression that with him a new epoch begins, a crisis in the religious history of Israel. The account given of Elijah, it is true, is adorned with much that is legendary; but the fact that tradition has sketched his image with so much that is stupendous and superhuman, and that such a garland of legends could be woven around him, is the clearest proof of his greatness which makes him tower above all his predecessors and contemporaries. Where smoke is, there fire must be, and where much smoke is, there the fire must be great. Let us try to sketch out a picture of Elijah, of his true importance and historical achievements.

It was a trying time. In the year 876 an Assyrian army had penetrated for the first time as far as Lebanon and the Mediterranean Sea, and had laid Israel under contribution. In addition, Israel had just had an unlucky struggle with the neighboring kingdom of Damascus, its hereditary foe. In this conjuncture, King Ahab assumed the reins of power.

Ahab, owing to his conflict with Elijah, is ranked among the biblical miscreants—but as unjustly so as Saul. Ahab was one of the best kings and mightiest rulers that Israel ever had, esteemed and admired by both friend and foe as a man of worth and character.

He was thoroughly equal to the situation, and after severe struggles raised Israel to a position which it had held under none of his predecessors. The only thing which he can be blamed for is his weakness towards his wife, the bigoted and intriguing Tyrian princess, Jezebel.

Jezebel's father, Ethbaal, had formerly been a priest of Baal, and had raised himself to the throne of Tyre by the murder of his predecessor. Ahab, now, in honor of his wife, caused a temple to be erected in Samaria to the Tyrian Baal. That Ahab extirpated, or wished to extirpate, from Israel the worship of Yahveh, is pure legend. The three children of Ahab and of Jezebel whose names we know, both his successors, Ahajiah and Jehoram, and the later queen of Judah, Athaljah, bear names compounded of Yahveh, and shortly before his death there lived in Samaria four hundred Yahveh prophets, who prophesied to the king whatever he wished. Ahab's doings in this matter are quite analogous to the building of the Greek Catholic chapel in the famous watering-place of Wiesbaden, because the first wife of the late Duke of Nassau was a Russian princess.

The supposed idolatry of Solomon is to be explained in the same manner. Solomon was the first who extended the intellectual horizon of Israel beyond the borders of Palestine, and opened the land to intellectual and commercial traffic with the outside world. In his capital, which he desired should become a metropolis, every one was to be saved after his own fashion, and for this reason Solomon built temples to the gods of all the nations who had dealings with Jerusalem.

No man, apparently, had taken offence at the action of Ahab, or had seen in it a transgression against the national Deity, until Elijah cried out to the people the following words, which are surely authentic: "How long will ye halt between two opinions? If Yahveh be God, serve him, but if Baal be God, serve him." Elijah was no opposer of Baal on grounds of principle; he travels in Phœnicia, the special home of Baal, and exhibits the power of his miracles in the service of a worshipper of Baal, the widow of Zarephath; but in Israel there was no room for Baal; there Yahveh alone was King and God. It is the energy and sensitiveness of his consciousness of God that rebels against the least suspicion of syncretism, and sees in it a scoffing and mockery of Yahveh, who will have His people exclusively for Himself. He who serves partly Baal and partly Yahveh is like, according to Elijah's drastic imagery, a man lame in both legs.

But another and more important point fell in the balance here. Hard by the palace of Ahab in Jezreel, Naboth the Jezreelite had a vineyard which the king wished to make into a garden of herbs. He offered Naboth, therefore, the worth of it in money, or, if he preferred, a better vineyard. But Naboth, with the proud joy of the true yeoman in his hereditary land, answers the king: "The Lord forbid it me that I should give the inheritance of my fathers unto thee." With these words the matter is at an end, so far as Ahab is concerned, but he cannot conceal his disappointment. Jezebel, his wife, hears of the matter, and says unto him the mocking and inciting words: "Dost thou now govern the Kingdom of Israel? I will give thee the vineyard of Naboth." Ahab let her have her will, and Jezebel's rule in Israel according to her views cost Ahab and his house their throne. False witnesses testified against Naboth, he was stoned to death as a blasphemer against God and the king, and his goods were confiscated.

In the ancient East, as to-day, such events were of every-day occurrence, accepted by everybody as a matter of course. The contemporaries of Ahab, however, saw in this deed something unheard of; they had the feeling as if heaven and earth would fall, since a king of Israel was capable of committing such a crime. Elijah made himself the mouthpiece of the general indignation.

On the following day, when the king arose to take possession of the vineyard, he meets there the mighty man, clothed in his hairy garment, who calls to him in a voice of thunder: "Thou who didst sell thyself to work wickedness! thus saith Yahveh: I have yesterday seen the blood of Naboth and of his children, and I will requite thee in this plat." Elijah does not announce the destruction of the ruling house on account of its idolatry, but as an act of justice. It was not the Tyrian Baal which overthrew the dynasty Omri, but the crime committed on a simple peasant.

According to the universal voice of tradition, Elijah achieved and attained nothing. But that is his highest praise and his greatest fame. For Elijah was a man of pure heart and of clean hands, who fought only with spiritual weapons. There exists no greater contrast than that between Elijah and the man looked upon as his heir and successor, Elisha. Tradition itself has felt this difference; the miracles narrated of Elisha, in so far as they are not pure imitations of Elijah's, all possess a grotesque, one might almost say, a vulgar, character: the sanctification and grandeur of Elijah are wanting throughout. Elisha had seen from his predecessor's example that nothing could be achieved with spiritual weapons; he became a demagogue and conspirator, a revolutionist and agitator. He incites one of the most contemptible characters known in the history of Israel, the cavalry officer Jehu, to smite the house of Ahab, and to set himself upon the throne of Israel. This came to pass. Elisha had attained his object, and the Tyrian Baal had disappeared out of Samaria, but Israel itself was brought to the verge of destruction. The reign of Jehu and of his son, Jehoahaz, is the saddest period that Israel ever passed through, and eighty years afterwards the prophet Hosea saw in the bloody deeds of Jehu an unatoned for guilt, that weighed down upon the kingdom and dynasty, and which could only be expiated by the fall of both.

In what, now, does the importance of Elijah consist?

Elijah is the first prophet in a truly Israelitic sense, differing from the later prophets only in that his efficacy, like that of Jesus of Nazareth, was entirely personal and in that he left nothing written. He saw that man does not live by bread alone, nor nations through sheer power. He considered Israel solely as the bearer of a higher idea. If the people became unfaithful to this idea, no external power could help them; for the nation bore in itself the germ of death. Israel was not to become a common nation like the others; it should serve Yahveh alone, so as to become a righteous and pure people.

Elijah was in holy earnest about this Mosaic thought; he measured his age and its events by this standard; he placed things temporal under an eternal point of view, and judged them accordingly. The crying evils existed plainly in the modes of worship and in the administration of the law. Undefiled worship and a righteous administration of the law are what God requires above all things. Here, if anywhere, it was to be shown whether Israel was in reality the people of God.

It is no accident that the first appearance of genuine prophecy in Israel coincided with the first advent of the Assyrians. Historical catastrophes have invariably aroused prophesying in Israel, and for this reason the prophets have been well called the storm-petrels of the world's history. This Amos has expressed in a highly characteristic manner, where he says: "Shall a trumpet be blown in the city and the people not be afraid? Shall there be evil in a city and the Lord hath not done it? Surely the Lord Yahveh will do nothing but he revealeth his secret unto his servants, the prophets. The Lion hath roared, who will not fear? The Lord God hath spoken, who can but prophesy?"

The prophet possesses the capacity of recognising God in history. He feels it when catastrophes are in the air. He stands on his watch-tower and spies out the signs of the times, so as to interpret them to his people, and to point out to them the right way, which will surely guide them out of all danger.

Moreover, the prophet is also the incorporate conscience of the nation, feeling all things and bringing all things to light that are rotten in the nation and displeasing to God. Micah has expressed this, in very apt terms, where he states his antithesis to the false prophets, as follows: "If a man walking in the spirit and falsehood do lie saying: I will prophesy unto thee of wine and strong drink; he shall even be the prophet of the people . . . [They are] the prophets that make my people err, that bite with their teeth and cry peace; and he that putteth not into their mouths they even prepare war against him . . . but truly I am full of power by the spirit of the Lord, and of judgment, and of might, to declare unto Jacob his transgression, and to Israel his sin."

That is the prophet of Israel, as he is in his true character and innermost significance: a man who has the power to look at temporal things under eternal points of view, who sees God's rule in all things, who knows, as the incorporate voice of God, how to interpret to his contemporaries the plan of God, and to direct them according to His will. This way alone leads to salvation. To reject it is certain destruction, be the outward appearance of the nation ever so imposing.

Of these genuine prophets of Israel, Elijah was the first, and therefore a personality that stood forth in his age in solitary grandeur, not understood, but an object of admiration to the latest generations, and the pioneer of a new epoch in the history of the religion of Israel.

All these men keep adding to the work of Moses; they build on the foundations which he laid. Without Moses the prophets would never have existed, and therefore they themselves have the feeling of bringing nothing absolutely new. But as faithful and just stewards they have put to interest the pound they inherited from Moses. The national religion founded by Moses became through the prophets the religion of the world. How this took place, in a marvellously organic development, the consideration of those prophets whose writings have been preserved, will show us.

AMOS.

NOTHING is more characteristic than the appearance of written prophecy in Israel.

It was at Bethel, at the Autumn festival. In that place where once Jacob saw in a dream the angels of God ascending and descending, where God had appeared to him and had blessed him, there was the sanctuary of the kingdom of Israel, the religious centre of the ten tribes. Here stood the revered image of the bull, under which symbol the God of Israel was worshipped. Here all Israel had gathered for thanksgiving and adoration, for festivity and sacrifice.

In distinct opposition to the harsh austerity and sombre rigor of the later Judaism, the worship of God in ancient Israel was of a thoroughly joyful and cheerful character. It was a conception utterly strange to the ancient Israelite that worship was instituted to restore the impaired relation of man to God, or that it was the office of sacrifice to bring about an atonement for sins. The ancient Israelite considered the service of God a rejoicing in God. In the sacrifice, of which

God received His appointed portion, whilst the sacrificer himself consumed the rest, he sat at the table with God, he was the guest of his God, and therefore doubly conscious of his union with Him. And as ancient Israel was a thoroughly cheerful and joyous people, its rejoicing in God bore, according to our ideas, many very worldly and unrighteous traits. Revelry and tumultuous carousing marked the festivals. As on the occasion of such an autumn festival at Shiloh, the mother of Samuel poured out her heart to God in silent prayer, Eli said unto her: "How long wilt thou be drunken? put away thy wine from thee." So that evidently drunken women were not seldom seen on such occasions. The prophet Isaiah gives us a still more drastic sketch of a celebration in the temple at Jerusalem, when he describes how all the tables were full of vomit and filthiness, so that there was no place clean. And even worse things, licentious debaucheries of the lowest sort, took place during these festivals.

The prophets recognised in these excrescences, and certainly most justly, remnants of Canaanite paganism. Israel had not only taken its sanctuaries from the Canaanites, but also its modes of worship. The contemporaries of Amos, however, considered this the correct and fitting worship of God, such as the God of Israel demanded from His people, and such as was pleasing unto Him.

In the year 760 such another feast was celebrated in Bethel. Revelry was the order of the day. And why should man not rejoice and give thanks to God? After a long period of direst tribulation and distress Israel had again raised itself to power. Its worst enemy, the kingdom of Damascus, had been decisively defeated, and was no longer dangerous. The neighboring nations had been subjected, and Jeroboam II. reigned over a kingdom which nearly attained the size and grandeur of the kingdom of David. The good old times of this greatest ruler of Israel seemed to have come again. Israel was the ruling nation between the Nile and Euphrates. And were not affairs in the interior of the kingdom as brilliant and stupendous as they had ever been? There were palaces of ivory in Samaria then, and houses of hewn stone without number, castles and forts, horses and chariots, power and pomp, splendor and riches, wherever one might turn. The rich lay on couches of ivory with damask cushions; daily they slew a fatted calf, drank the most costly wines, and anointed themselves with precious oils. All in all, it was a period in which to live was a joy. Accordingly, the feast was celebrated with unwonted splendor, and untold sacrifices were offered. Men lived in the consciousness that God was on their side, and they were grateful to Him.

But just as the festival mirth was at its highest, it was suddenly interrupted. An unknown, plain-looking man of the people forced his way through the crowd of merry-makers. A divine fire gleamed in his eyes, a holy gravity suffused his countenance. With shy, involuntary respect room is made for him, and before the people well know what has happened, he has drowned and brought to silence the festive songs by the piercing mournful cry of his lamentation. Israel had a special form of poetry for its funeral dirge, a particular melodious cadence, which reminded every hearer of the most earnest moments of his life, as he had stood, weeping, for the last time at the bier of his father, his mother, wife, or some beloved child, and this form was adopted repeatedly by the prophets with great effect. Such a dirge does the strange man now intone in the sanctuary at Bethel. It is a dirge over Israel; he shouts it among the merry-makers that are crowded before him:

> "The virgin of Israel is fallen,
> She shall no more rise,
> She is forsaken upon her land,
> There is none to raise her up."

The assembly is seized with astonishment and consternation. Men inquire who the strange speaker is, and are told that he is called Amos, a herdsman of Tekoa, who has uttered such blasphemies several times before. For to predict the destruction of God's own people was the acme of blasphemy; it was the same as saying that either God was not willing or that He had not the power to protect and save His people; it was equivalent to prophesying God's own destruction; for God Himself perished with the people who served and honored Him. Yet this wondrous prophet adds to his blasphemy, insanity. It is God Himself who destroys His people Israel, Who must destroy it. He has sworn it by His holiness, by Himself, that the end is come over His people Israel.

No long time elapsed before Amaziah the priest came up and addressed the bold speaker in these words: "O thou seer, go, flee thee away into the land of Judah and there eat bread and prophesy there : But prophesy not again at Bethel ; for it is the King's chapel, and the King's court."

Then Amos answered : "I was no prophet, neither was I a prophet's son ; but I was an herdman and a gatherer of sycomore fruit : And the Lord took me as I followed the flock, and the Lord said unto me, Go, prophesy unto my people Israel." And he now concludes his general warning of evil with a personal threat to the high-priest : "Thy wife shall be an harlot in the city, and thy sons and thy daughters shall fall by the sword, and thy land shall be divided by line, and thou shalt die in a polluted land."

After Amos had fulfilled the divine charge, he returned home to his sheep and to his sycamores. But feeling that what he had prophesied was not for the present, nor for those immediately concerned, but spoken for all time, he wrote down his prophecies and left them as an imperishable monument.

Now, how did Amos arrive at this conviction, which reversed everything that at that time seemed to be the destiny of Israel. When he pictures to himself the overthrow of Israel, the conquest and destruction of its army, the plundering and desolation of its land, and the captivity and transportation of its people by a foreign foe, he is thinking, of course, of the Assyrians, although he never mentions the name. This lowering thundercloud had repeatedly flashed its lightnings over Israel's horizon, first in the year 876, and in the succeeding century ten times at least. At last, in 767, the Assyrian hosts had penetrated as far as Lebanon and the Mediterranean Sea, spreading terror and devastation everywhere. But at the time in question the danger was not very imminent. The Assyrian empire was then in a state of the uttermost confusion and impotence. Amos's conviction, accordingly, was no political forecast. Moreover, the most important and most unintelligible point remains unexplained on such an assumption. Why was this condemnation an absolute necessity, willed and enforced by God Himself? This the prophet foresaw from his mere sense of justice.

In Amos we have, so to speak, the incorporation of the moral law. God is a God of justice; religion the moral relation of man to God—not a comfortable pillow, but an ethical exaction. Israel had faith in its God, He would not leave his people in the lurch, but would assist them and rescue them from all calamity. This singular relation of Israel to its God, Amos acknowledges: "You only have I known of all the families of the earth." But what is his conclusion? "Therefore I will punish you for all your iniquities."

Amos had already clearly perceived what a greater than he clothed in these words: "To whom much has been given, of him will much be required." The outer relation in itself is entirely worthless. "Are ye not as children of the Ethiopians unto me, O children of Israel?" says God through Amos. And also God's special marks of favor, in having led Israel out of Egypt and through the desert, prove nothing; for He had also done the same for Israel's most bitter enemies. "Have I not brought up Israel out of the land of Egypt? and the Philistines from Caphtor, and the Syrians from Kir?"

True, the people are pious after their fashion; they cannot do enough in the matter of feasts and sacrifices. But all this appears to the prophet merely as an attempt to bribe the just judge, after a manner very prevalent at the time. Says God through Amos:

"I hate, I despise your feast days, and I will not smell in your solemn assemblies. Though ye offer me burnt offerings and your meat offerings, I will not accept them, neither will I regard the peace offerings of your fat beasts. Take thou away from me the noise of thy songs; for I will not hear the melody of thy viols. But let judgment run down as waters, and righteousness as a mighty stream." "Seek me and ye shall live. . . . Hate the evil and love the good and establish judgment in the gate."

But it is just in what God here demands that Israel is totally wanting. Amos sees about him rich voluptuaries and debauchees, who derive the means of carrying on their sinful lives by shameful extortion and the scandalous oppression of the poor and the weak, thereby storing up in their palaces oppression and tyranny. Justice is turned to wormwood and righteousness thrown to the earth; a bribe is taken against the just, and the poor sold for a pair of shoes. And the worst of all is, that they neither know nor feel how wicked and corrupt they are; they live carelessly and listlessly on, and have no conception of the instability of all things.

Yet no particular insight or revelation is necessary. Amos can call upon the heathen, the Philistines, and the Egyptians to bear witness to God's dealings with Israel. Even these heathen who know not God and His commandments must see that in Samaria things are done which cry out to heaven, and that Israel is ripe for death. Therefore must God Himself as an atonement for his despised sanctity and justice destroy his people. He says:

"The end for my people Israel is at hand, I can no longer forgive."

The blooming pink on the cheek of the virgin Israel is not for the prophet a sign of health, but the hectic flush of one diseased and hastening to her end. In all the noise and tumult, the hurry and bustle, his keen ear detects the death-rattle, and he intones Israel's funeral dirge. And history has justified him.

Forty years afterwards the kingdom of Israel was swept away, and its people carried into captivity.

But, you may ask, is there anything so wonderful in all this? Are not these very commonplace truths that are offered us here? To think so, would be a serious error. As a fact, the progress which the religion of Israel made in and through Amos cannot be too highly rated. In Amos it breaks for the first time through the bonds of nationality and becomes a universal religion instead of the religion of a single people. In analysing the relationship of God to Israel, or at least in recognising it as morally conditioned, which by the fulfilment of the moral conditions could just as well be discharged by any other people, he gave a philosophical foundation to religion, which rendered it possible that the religion of Israel and the God of Israel should not become implicated in the fall of Israel, but could be developed all the more grandly. The fall of the people of Israel was the victory of God, the triumph of justice and truth over sin and deception. That which had destroyed every other religion could now only strengthen the religion of Israel.

This progress shows itself most strongly in the conception of God. Ancient Israel had no monotheism, in the strict scientific sense. The gods of the heathen were looked upon as real beings, as actual gods, who in their spheres were as powerful as the God of Israel in His. That had now to be otherwise. Right and justice exist beyond the boundaries of Israel; they reach even further than the might of the Assyrians. For right is right everywhere, and wrong is everywhere wrong. If the God of Israel was the God of justice, then His kingdom extended as far as justice did,—then He was the God of the world, as Amos expressed it by the name he framed for God, Zebaoth, the Lord of hosts, the God of all power and might in heaven and on earth.

National boundaries fell before this universal power of justice. When the Moabites burnt to lime the bones of an Edomite king they drew down upon themselves the judgment and punishment of the God of Israel. Justice and righteousness are the only reality in heaven and on earth. Thus through Amos the God of Israel, as the God of justice and righteousness, becomes the God of the entire world, and the religion of this God a universal religion.

Amos is one of the most marvellous and incomprehensible figures in the history of the human mind, the pioneer of a process of evolution from which a new epoch of humanity dates. And here again we see that the most important and imposing things are the simplest and apparently the most easily understood.

HOSEA.

WITH all due acknowledgment of the greatness of Amos, it is impossible to acquit him of a certain narrow-mindedness. His God is essentially a criminal judge, inspiring fear but not love; and on fear alone neither the heart of man nor religion can exist. With the execution of the judgment matters are at an end, so far as Amos is concerned. What was to take place afterwards, he does not ask. This was soon felt as a defect, and a reconciliatory conclusion was appended to the Book of Amos, which contains little of his ideas, and is at variance in all points with his doctrines. The real complement of Amos is found, marvellously developed, in Hosea, the prophet who came after him.

To Amos's proposition, "God is justice," Hosea adds: "God is love." Not as if Hosea were any less severe in his judgment of the evils of his people; on the contrary, he shows himself even more deeply affected by them, and his descriptions are far more sombre and ominous than those of Amos. But Hosea cannot rest content with a negation. For God is not a man, whose last word is anger and passion. He is the Holy One, the Merciful One, whom pity overcomes. He cannot cast aside the people whom He once loved. He will draw them to Himself, improve them, educate them. God is a kind Father, who punishes His child with a bleeding heart, for its own good, so that He may afterwards enfold it all the more warmly in His arms. Whilst in Amos the ethical element almost entirely predominates, in Hosea the religious element occupies the foreground. He and his intellectual and spiritual compeer, Jeremiah, were men of emotion, the most intense and the most deeply religious of all the prophets of Israel.

The manner in which Hosea was made aware of his calling is highly interesting and significant, and is a fresh proof of how pure and genuine human sentiment always leads to God. Family troubles bred prophecy in Hosea. He took to himself a wife. Her name and that of her father lead us to conclude that she was of low birth, a child of the people. We can easily understand how this serious, thoughtful man was attracted by the natural freshness and grace of this simple maiden. But when married she renders him deeply unhappy, and he had finally to admit that he had wasted his love on one unworthy, on a profligate woman. We cannot clearly make out whether the woman forsook him, or whether he cast her away. But now something incredible takes place. He, the deeply injured husband, cannot help regretting his wife. Could the innermost and purest feeling of his heart have been only self-deception? At one time she loved him. And Hosea feels himself responsible for her who was his wife. Was it not possible to wake the better self of the woman again? When the smothering ashes had been cleared away, could not the spark, which he cannot consider to have died out, spring up into a bright and pure flame? That was possible only through self-denying and tender-hearted love. Such love could not fail, in the end, to evoke a genuine response. He must try again this faithless woman, must have her near him. He takes her back into his house. He cannot reinstate her at once into the position and rights of a wife; she must first pass through a severe and hard period of probation; but if she goes through this probation, if she yields to the severe yet mild discipline of the husband who still loves her, then he will wed her afresh in love and trust, and nothing again shall rend asunder this new covenant.

Hosea recognises in this relation of his wife an image of the relation of God to Israel. God has chosen the poor, despised Israelites, the slaves of the Egyptians, to be His people; has allied Himself with them in love and faith, showered His blessings upon the nation, miraculously guided it, and finally made it great and mighty. And all these mercies are requited by Israel with the blackest ingratitude; its service of God is, in the eyes of the prophet, a worship of Baal, a mockery of the holy God, whom it knows not, and of whom it does not want to know; and therefore He must give it over to perdition. But for God this judgment is no personal object. He wishes thereby to lead these foolish and blinded hearts to reflexion and to self-knowledge. When they learn to pray in distress, when they humbly turn again to God with the open confession of their sins, then will He turn to them again, then will He accept into grace those fallen away, then will they be His people, who are now not His people, and He will be their God. Right and justice, grace and pity, love and faith, will He bring to them as the blessings and gifts of the new covenant, and they will acknowledge Him and become His willing and obedient children. He will be to Israel as the dew, and Israel shall grow as the lily and blossom out as the olive-tree, and stand there in the glory and scent of Lebanon.

God is love. Hosea recognised this, because he bore love in his heart, because it was alive in him; love which is long-suffering and kind, which seeketh not her own, is not easily provoked, which beareth all things, believeth all things, hopeth all things, endureth all things, the love which never faileth. When we consider that all this was absolutely new, that those thoughts in which humanity has been educated and which have consoled it for nearly three thousand years, were first spoken by Hosea, we must reckon him among the greatest religious geniuses which the world has ever produced. Among the prophets of Israel, Jeremiah alone can bear comparison with him, and even here we feel inclined to value Hosea higher, as the forerunner and pioneer.

Why is it that Hosea is so often misconceived in this, his great importance? He has not rendered it easy for us to do him justice, for his book is unusually obscure and difficult. It is in a way more than any other book individual and subjective. What Hosea gives us are really monologues, the ebullitions of a deeply moved heart, torn by grief, in all its varying moods and sentiments. Like the fantasies of one delirious, the images and thoughts push and pursue one another. But it is exactly this subjectivity and this individuality which gives to the Book of Hosea its special charm and irresistible efficacy. He is the master of heart-born chords, which for power and fervor are possessed by no other prophet. Let me quote, in Hosea's own words, an especially characteristic passage, a masterpiece of his book.

"When Israel was a child, I loved him and called him as my son out of Egypt. But the more I called the more they went from me; they sacrificed unto Baalim and burned incense to graven images. I taught Ephraim also to walk, taking him in my arms. But they knew not that I meant good with them. I drew them with cords of a man, with bands of love; and I was to them as they that take off the yoke on their jaws, and I laid meat unto them. Yet they will return into the land of Egypt, and Asshur be their king. Of me they will know nothing. So shall the sword abide in their cities, destroy their towers, and devour their strongholds. My people are bent to backsliding from me; when called on from on high, none looketh upwards. How shall I give thee up, Ephraim? How shall I deliver thee, Israel? Shall I make thee as Admah? Shall I set thee as Zeboim? My heart is turned within me, my compassion is cramped together. I will not execute the fierceness of mine anger. I will not return to destroy thee Ephraim, for I am God and not man; the Holy One in the midst of thee. I cannot come to destroy."

Thus is love, grace, mercy, ever the last word: for God is love. Thus religion becomes an act of love. God calls for love, not sacrifice, knowledge of God, not burnt offerings; and acquires thus a power of intimacy that till then was unknown. That dear, comforting phrase, "the Lord thy God," which places every individual man in a personal relation of love with God, was coined by Hosea, and is first found in his book Even the requirement of being born again, of having to become completely new, in order to be really a child of God, can be found in Hosea. He is the first who demands that God shall not be worshipped by images, and pours out his bitterest scorn on the "calves" of Dan and Bethel, as he dares to name the old, venerated bull-symbols. In fact, he demands a rigorous separation of the worship of God from the worship of nature. Everything that is contradictory to the real holy and spiritual nature of God is paganism

and must be done away with, **were it ten times** a venerable and traditional custom.

That this man, so apparently a man of emotion, governed entirely by his moods, and driven helplessly hither and thither by them, should have possessed a formal theological system, which has exercised an immeasurable influence on future generations, is a phenomenon of no slight significance. To prove this statement would require too much time and the discussion of details. (But it is not too much to say that the entire faith and theology of later Israel grew out of Hosea, that all its characteristic views and ideas are to be first found in his book.)

Hosea was a native of the northern part of the nation, its last and noblest offshoot. He wrote his book between 738 and 735 B. C., about twenty-five years after the appearance of Amos. We already know from the short accounts in the Book of Kings that this was a period of anarchy and dissolution; Hosea's book transplants us to this time, and allows us to see in the mirror of the prophet's woe-torn heart the whole life of this period.

It is a horrible panorama that unfolds itself before our eyes. One king murders the other; God gives him in his wrath and takes him away in his displeasure; for none can help, but all are torn away and driven about by the whirlpool of events, as a log upon the waters. So hopeless are matters that the prophet can pray, God should give to Ephraim a miscarrying womb and dry breasts, so that fresh offerings of calamity and misery should not be born. In such a state of affairs the thought strikes the prophet, that the whole state and political life is an evil, an opposition to God, a rebellion against Him who is the only Lord and King of Israel, and who will have men entirely for himself. In the hoped-for future time of bliss, when all things are such as God wishes them, there will be no king and no princes, no politics, no alliances, no horses and chariots, no war and no victory. What is usually known as the *theocracy* of the Old Testament, was created by Hosea, as the direct outcome of those distressful days.

As a man of sorrows, he was naturally not spared a personal martyrdom. He fulfils his mission in the midst of ridicule and contumely, amidst enmity and danger to his life. He occasionally gives us a sketch of this in his book: "The days of visitation are come, the days of recompense are come: Israel shall know it!" And the people shout back mockingly: "The prophet is a fool, the spiritual man is mad." Hosea takes up their words and answers:

"Verily I am mad, but on account of the multitude of thine iniquity and the multitude of the persecution."

"The snares of the fowler threaten destruction to the prophet in all his ways; even in the house of his God have they dug a deep pit for him."

We know not if Hosea survived the overthrow of Israel. His grave, still regarded as a sanctuary, is shown in Eastern Jordan, on the top of Mount Hosea, Dschebel Oscha, about three miles north of es-Salt, from where we can obtain one of the most beautiful views of Palestine.

ISAIAH.

IN THE year 722 B. C. Israel disappears, and Judah succeeds as its heir. From the time of Hosea prophecy has its existence wholly on the soil of Judah. At the head of these Judaic prophets stands Isaiah, who began his work shortly after the completion of the Book of Hosea. He is distinguished from both his predecessors by his personality and whole style of action. Whilst Amos only rages and punishes, Hosea only weeps and hopes, Isaiah is a thoroughly practical and positive character, who feels the necessity of influencing personally the destinies of his people. Evidently belonging to the highest classes—Jewish tradition makes him a priest of the King's house—he possessed and made use of his power and influence. Seated at the tiller, he guides by the divine compass the little ship of his fatherland through the rocks and breakers of a wild and stormy period.

It was the most critical period of the whole history of Judah. The question was, To be or not to be? If Judah weathered this crisis and held out for over a century, it is essentially due to the endeavors of the prophet Isaiah who knew how to make clear to his contemporaries the wondrous plan of God. In Isaiah we find for the first time a clearly grasped conception of universal history. Nothing takes place on earth but it is directed by a supramundane holy will, and has as its ulterior object the honor of God. God is all, man is nothing—thus perhaps the theology of Isaiah could be most tersely and clearly stated. God is supramundane, the all-powerful, who fills heaven and earth, the Holy One of Israel, as Isaiah loves to call Him, who proves His sanctity by His justice. Man is in His hand as clay in the hand of the potter. Even the powerful Assyrians are but the rod of His wrath, whom He at once destroys on their presuming to become more than a mere tool in the hands of God. Pride, therefore, is the special sin of man, as where he arrogates to himself the honor and glory which belong to God alone.

In one of his earliest prophecies Isaiah bursts forth like a thunderstorm over everything great and lofty that men possess and men produce. All this will be mercilessly levelled to the ground—"the lofty looks of man shall be humbled, and the haughtiness of men shall be bowed down, and the Lord alone shall be exalted in that day." On the other hand, the true virtue of man is loyal confidence in God and submission to his will. "In quietness and rest shall ye be saved; in submission and confidence shall be your strength," so does he preach to his people.

This guidance of the history of the world by a supramundane holy will, as the fulfilment of its own honor, is what Isaiah repeatedly terms "the work of God." It is true, this work is singular, this plan is wondrous, but man must accept it and submit to it. Their blindness to it, their wilfully closing their eyes against it, is the severest reproof which the prophet brings against his people. But let us follow up his work in its single stages and see if we can understand it.

At the opening of Isaiah's theology we find the thought, "A remnant shall return." Thus had he named his eldest son, just as Hosea had given significant names to his children, and made them in a certain sense living witnesses of his prophetic preaching. Like Amos, Isaiah considers the judgment as unavoidable, but like Hosea he sees in the judgment not the end but the beginning of the true salvation. Yet in the manner in which he thinks out the realisation of this salvation, Isaiah goes his own way. He cannot think of his people as only a rabble of godless evil-doers; there must be some among them susceptible of good, and whom one can imagine as worthy of becoming citizens of the future kingdom of God, and those are the "remnant." This remnant is the "holy seed" from which the future Israel shall burst forth under God's care. Thus Isaiah sees the object of the judgment to be, the rooting out of the godless and the sinners, so that this noble remnant, which is left over, shall continue alone in the field and develop free and unhindered. And this future kingdom of God Isaiah can only picture to himself under a mundane form. This is his principal contrast to Hosea, the opposition of the Judæan to the Israelite.

In Judah, where the supremacy of the House of David had never been seriously opposed, a benign stability had prevailed in all affairs and a doctrine of legitimacy had been established, owing to a lack of which Israel was incessantly disturbed and hurried on from revolution to revolution, from anarchy to anarchy. These inestimable mundane blessings the prophet is anxious shall not be wanting in the future kingdom of God. We find in his work a very remarkable passage in which he places a religious valuation on patriotism, and acknowledges it to be both a gift and the working of the spirit of God for men to fight valiantly for their country and to repel the enemy from its imperilled borders. The future kingdom of God shall also have its judges and officials, and above all, at its head an earthly king of the House of David. But this earthly king will rule over a kingdom of peace and justice. Then will all the harnesses of the proud warriors, and the blood-stained cloaks of the soldiers be consumed as fuel of the fire. And in their place the government will be on the shoulders of a child, who shall be called "Wonderful Counsellor, the Mighty God, the Everlasting Father, the Prince of Peace." Of the increase of peace there will be no end, and the throne of David will be established on judgment and justice for ever and ever.

And again most beautifully in another passage, which I cannot refrain from quoting in its own words :

"And there shall come forth a sprig out of the stem of Jesse and a branch shall grow out of his roots ; and the spirit of the Lord shall rest upon him, the spirit of wisdom and understanding, the spirit of counsel and might, the spirit of knowledge and of the fear of the Lord ; the delight of whose life shall be the fear of the Lord. And he shall not judge after the sight of his eyes, neither reprove after the hearing of his ears. But with righteousness shall he judge the poor and reprove with equity for the oppressed of the earth ; and he shall smite the tyrant with the rod of his mouth, and with the breath of his lips shall he slay the wicked. And righteousness shall be the girdle of his loins, and faithfulness the girdle of his reins. The wolf also shall dwell with the lamb, and the leopard shall lie down with the kid ; and the calf and the young lion and the fatling together ; and a little child shall lead them. And the cow and the bear shall feed ; their young ones shall lie down together ; and the lion shall eat straw like the ox. And the sucking child shall play on the hole of the asp, and the weaned child shall put his hand on the cockatrice' den. They shall not hurt nor destroy in all my holy mountain ; for the earth shall be full of the knowledge of the Lord, as the waters cover the sea."

How, now, shall this last design of the divine government of the world be fulfilled? The mission of Isaiah begins apparently with a shrill dissonance. As he receives the call and consecration to the office of prophet in the year of the death of Uzziah, 736 B.C., God speaks to him: "Go and tell this people, Hear ye indeed but understand not; and see ye indeed but perceive not! Make the heart of this people fat, and make their ears heavy, and shut their eyes; lest they see with their eyes, and hear with their ears, and understand with their heart, and convert, and be healed."

These words sound terrible, I might almost say godless, but they contain nevertheless a deep truth. Isaiah has clearly recognised that man can and dare not be indifferent to the good. Either he bows to the good and it becomes a blessing to him, or he hardens his heart against it, and it becomes to him a double curse. The nation as a whole is neither ripe nor ready for the future kingdom of God. And since the judgment is the necessary transition to salvation, since the quicker the judgment comes, the quicker salvation can be effected, therefore it is to the interest both of God and Israel if the sins of the latter shall speedily reach a point where judgment must ensue.

Uzziah was a vigorous ruler, whose reign of fifty-two years was a period of power and splendor for Judah. This, however, was entirely changed when in the year 735 B. C. his grandson Ahaz ascended the throne. This young monarch was a perfect type of the Oriental despot, capricious, extravagant, profligate, cruel, acknowledging only his own will as the highest law. In his reign just such conditions prevailed in the kingdom as are described in Israel by Amos and Hosea. Outside troubles were soon to be added to this inner dissolution. Whilst the great Assyrian conqueror Tiglath-Pileser already hovered over their heads like a lowering thundercloud, the small kingdoms had in their confusion nothing better to do than to fall to blows with one another. Rezin of Damascus and Pekah of Israel took advantage of Ahaz's weak and unpopular government and allied themselves in an attack on Judah, which they drove to such sore straits that even a siege of Jerusalem seemed imminent. Ahaz helped himself out of this dilemma by taking a desperate step. He placed himself and his kingdom voluntarily under the protection of Assyria as the price of being rescued by the Assyrians from his enemies.

Isaiah evidently knew of these machinations. One day as Ahaz was inspecting the works for the defence and fortification of Jerusalem, he publicly stepped in front of the king and implored him to rely on his good cause, and to have confidence in God, who would surely help him. As Ahaz hesitates, Isaiah says to him: "Ask thee a sign from the Lord thy God, ask it either in the depth or in the height above." Tremendous words, a belief in God of such intensity as to appear to us men of modern times fanatical. We can hardly take umbrage, therefore, at the remark of one of the most brilliant modern interpreters of Isaiah, that the prophet had every reason for being grateful to Ahaz for his unbelief, in that he did not take him at his word and ask for the sign. And now with flaming eyes Isaiah discloses to him his shortsightedness. The means will indeed help, but at a high cost, for the decisive struggle between Assyria and Egypt will then have to be fought out on the soil of Judah, and thereby the country will be shaved with the razor that has been hired, namely, by them beyond the river Euphrates, and converted into a desert and a wilderness.

After that Isaiah has made Ahaz and his son responsible for all the consequences by their want of trust in God, and, knowing full well that all public labor would now be in vain, he temporarily abandons the scene, and begins a more silent task. He sets to work to form and educate the remnant which shall be left and on which depends the hope of Israel. He gathers about him a band of kindred hearts, whom he names disciples of God, "to bind up the testimony and to seal the law" for him and them.

"I am thy son and thy slave. Come up and save me from the King of Damascus and from the King of Israel," was the fatal message sent by Ahaz to Tiglath-Pileser, who did not wait to be twice summoned, but came at once. Israel was conquered in 734, King Pekah executed, and two-thirds of the country annexed. In 732, after three years' hard fighting, Damascus also succumbed to the Assyrian arms. King Rezin was executed and his land converted into an Assyrian province.

One may think of Ahaz as one likes. But political foresight he certainly possessed, as the issue proved. By his remaining loyal and unwavering in his unsought submission to Assyria, he brought it about that whilst one after another of the neighboring kingdoms sank, whilst war and uproar, murder and plunder raged about him, Judah remained quiet, a peaceful island on a storm-tossed sea.

Ahaz died in the year 720 B.C., and was succeeded by his son Hezekiah. Hezekiah was of a weak and wavering character. Under him the national party, which wished, with the assistance of Egypt, to shake off the Assyrian yoke, obtained the supremacy. Here, again, was work for Isaiah. At that time Assyria under Sargon, one of the most powerful of warrior-kings, and, what we must also not overlook, one of the noblest and most sympathetic of all the Assyrian rulers, was celebrating her greatest triumphs, winning her most brilliant victories, and achieving her most marvellous successes. According to Isaiah, that could only have been accomplished through God, or suffered by Him; and therefore he drew the conclusion, that in conformity with God's plan the Assyrian's rôle was not yet exhausted, that God still had need of him and had yet greater things in store for him. To rise against the Assyrian was rebellion against the will of God, and so Isaiah did all in his power to keep Judah quiet and guard it against foolish enterprises.

When in the year 711 B.C. the excitement was at

its highest, and men were on the verge of yielding to the siren voice of Egypt, Isaiah appeared publicly in the despicable garb of a prisoner of war, as a sign that the prisoners of Egypt and Ethiopia would be led away captives in this apparel by the Assyrians. But to forestall the thought that the overpowering advance of the Assyrian Empire was after all a serious danger to Judah, which prudence and self-preservation bade the nation unconditionally to guard against, Isaiah at this critical period establishes a dogma, which was to be of the uttermost importance for all future ages—the dogma of the inviolability of Mount Zion. There God has His dwelling on earth, His habitation; whosoever touched this, touched the personal property of God. And such an attack God could not permit; even the mighty Assyrian would dash himself to pieces against the hill of Zion, if in his impious presumption he dared to stretch out his hand against it. Isaiah really succeeded in subduing the excitement. Jerusalem remained quiet and no further steps were taken.

In the year 705 Sargon died, probably murdered by his son and successor Sennacherib. Everywhere did men rejoice, that the rod of the oppressor was broken, and they now prepared themselves with all their might to shake off the yoke. Isaiah remained firm in his warnings to undertake nothing and to leave everything in the hands of God.

This was not cowardice. On the contrary, it was a sublime consciousness of strength, the sentiment of being in God's hand, of being safe and protected by Him. This is proved by a very characteristic passage, which is one of the most powerful in all Isaiah. An embassy had come from Ethiopia to Jerusalem to solicit an alliance against Assyria; Isaiah says: "Return to your country. All ye inhabitants of the world and dwellers on the earth, see ye, when he lifteth up an ensign on the mountains, and when he bloweth a trumpet, hear ye. For so the Lord said unto me, I will take my rest, and I will consider in my dwelling-place like a clear heat upon herbs and like a cloud of dew in the heat of harvest. For afore the harvest when the bud is perfect and the sour grape is ripening in the flower, he shall both cut off the sprigs with pruning hooks, and take away and cut down the branches. They shall be left together with the fowls of the mountains, and to the beasts of the earth; and the fowls shall summer upon them, and all the beasts of the earth shall winter upon them." Then will the Ethiopians also bow down to the God, who is enthroned on Zion.

Here God plays with the Assyrian as a wild beast with his prey. He lets him have his own way, appears even to encourage him; but at the right moment He has only to strike out to stretch him lifeless on the ground.

This time, however, Isaiah was unable to stem the rising current of enthusiastic patriotism. In spite of his efforts an alliance with Ethiopia and Egypt was concluded, and Hezekiah together with all the small rulers of the neighboring lands, openly rebelled against the mighty Assyrian monarch.

Isaiah's position at this period is very curious, and apparently a very contradictory one. Nowhere does he oppose his people with greater harshness, never did he utter bitterer truths, or hurl more terrible threats against them; yet despite all he remains unmoved in his assurance that God will save Jerusalem, and not suffer it to fall into the hands of the heathen. And wonderful to say, his prediction is fulfilled!

In the year 701 Sennacherib approached with a mighty army. Egypt and Ethiopia were beaten, and Judæa horribly desolated. The Assyrians robbed and plundered forty-six cities, and drove 200,150 men out of this small land of not over 1500 square miles into captivity. But the waves actually broke against the walls of Jerusalem. The Assyrians withdrew without having accomplished their object. In the direst moment of trouble God triumphed over them and protected his city. The fate to which twenty-one years previously Israel and Samaria had succumbed, did not befall Judah and Jerusalem.

We can well imagine how the wonderful fulfilment of his prophecy must have increased the authority of the prophet. God Himself had imprinted the seal of His approval on the words of Isaiah. And this man, ever restlessly active for the welfare of his people, at once turned his success to practical profit. The Book of Kings tells us that Hezekiah reformed the worship of the nation and abolished the worst idolatrous practices in the temple at Jerusalem. We must surely imagine Isaiah as the motive power in this reform, and as the date of its carrying out we should most naturally select the time succeeding the wonderful preservation of Jerusalem. Thus with Isaiah prophecy had become a power which exerted a decisive influence over the destinies of the people, and brought it safely and surely to blessing and to salvation.

We know nothing of the last days of Isaiah. The legend that he suffered martyrdom at an advanced age, is wholly unfounded, and in itself highly improbable.

With Isaiah sank into the grave the greatest classic of Israel. Never did the speech of Canaan pour forth with more brilliant splendor and triumphant beauty than from his lips. He has a strength and power of language, a majesty and sublimity of expression, an inexhaustible richness of fitting and stirring imagery, that overwhelms the reader, nay, fairly bewilders him.

This and the circumstance that too little is known of his predecessors, is probably the reason why Isaiah is often overrated. He was certainly one of the greatest men of Israel. But the ideas at the basis of his prophecies are already found in Amos and Hosea. What he added of his own was a two-edged sword. A hundred years later Jeremiah had to wage a life and death struggle against them; for wrongly extended and exaggerated, those very ideas ultimately brought about the destruction of Jerusalem and Judah.

In religious depth and fervor Isaiah is far surpassed by Hosea. We do not find in the titanic pathos of Isaiah the touching, heart-born tones that sob out and caress us in the Book of Hosea. His historical and religious importance lies in something quite different, namely, in that he saved Judah, and in doing so saved religion.

The Israelites, who were carried away into Assyrian captivity in 722, are untraceably lost. They were absorbed by their conquerors. Had the same fate befallen Judah and Jerusalem, they too would have disappeared. That their ruin was delayed a century and time gained in which religion could firmly establish itself and strike deep roots, so as to survive the overthrow of Judah and Jerusalem, was Isaiah's work and merit.

In conclusion I should like to make some brief mention of a contemporary of Isaiah who forms an exceedingly curious contrast to him—Micah the Morasthite. In him Amos lives again. Like Amos, a dweller in the country, and a man of the people, his straightforward and lively sense of justice suffered itself to be neither silenced nor repressed. A moral indignation, truly awe-inspiring, overpowers him at all he sees and experiences. Especially the sins of the nobility of Jerusalem, those unscrupulous bloodsuckers and despoilers of the people, who stopped at naught if they had but the power, are so atrocious that they can only be atoned for by the destruction of Jerusalem. Therefore he calls to them:

"Hear this ye heads of the house of Jacob and princes of the house of Israel that abhor judgment and pervert all equity. Who build up Zion with blood and Jerusalem with iniquity. The heads thereof judge for reward, and the priests thereof teach for hire, and the prophets thereof divine for money—and yet do they lean upon God and say, Is not God among us? none evil can come upon us. Therefore shall Zion for your sake be plowed as a field and Jerusalem shall become heaps, and the mountain of the temple as the high places of the forest."

A strange contrast between the two contemporaries. One cannot help thinking that Micah is in direct controversy with Isaiah. History has proved both to be right. At first Isaiah was victorious. But one hundred and fifteen years after Jerusalem was rescued from the hands of Sennacherib, the prophecy of Micah was fulfilled. Jerusalem became a heap of ruins, the temple a smoking pile, and the people were led away into far captivity.

THE REACTION AGAINST THE PROPHETS.

IT WAS Hosea who first perceived that the traditional system of worship, which in his eyes was arrant paganism, constituted the real cancer that was eating the life of Israel. Isaiah shared his view, and, being of a practical nature, acted upon it. The prophecy of Israel openly and hostilely attacks the religion of the people and endeavors to mould it according to the prophetic ideal. That was no easy task and had, in the nature of the case, to meet with bitter and fanatical opposition. We men of modern times can scarcely appreciate what religion means to a primitive people, how it governs and enters into all their relations and becomes the pulse and motive power of their whole life. On the other hand, the power of custom in religion cannot be too highly rated. Tradition is considered sacred because it is tradition. The heart clings to it. The solemn moments of life are inseparably bound up with it, and every alteration of it appears as blasphemy, as an insult to God.

And now let us consider the feelings of the people of Judah towards the reforms proposed and inaugurated by Isaiah. The ancient and honored relics, which could be traced back to the Patriarchs and to Moses, before which David had knelt, which from time immemorial had been to every Israelite the most sacred and beloved objects on earth, should now of a sudden, to quote Isaiah, be considered as filth to be cast to moles and bats, because a few fanatics in Jerusalem did not find them to their taste! Now indeed, if the new God whom the prophets preached (for thus he must have appeared to the people) had only been more powerful than the older, whom their fathers had worshipped, if things had only gone on better—well and good. But there was no trace of this.

So long as we were confined solely to the Old Testament for our knowledge of Jewish history, it was supposed naturally enough that with the futile attack on Jerusalem in the year 701 the Assyrian domination in Judah was broken for all time, and that Judah had again become free. But that is not the case. As a matter of fact the Assyrian power only attained to the zenith of its glory under the two successors of Sennacherib, Esarhaddon and Asurbanipal. It is true that Sennacherib did not again enter Palestine, as he had enough to do in the neighborhood of his own capital, and it may be that for a short time a certain respite was gained. But Israel remained as before an Assyrian province, and Judah as before the vassal of the Assyrian monarch, having yearly to send a tribute to Nineveh. In fact, the Assyrian rule became more and more oppressive. Esarhaddon had laid the keystone in the Assyrian domination of the world by his conquest of Egypt. Thrice in rapid succession had the Assyrian army forced its way to Thebes, and Assyrian viceroys governed Egypt as an Assyrian province. Asurbanipal had also fought in Egypt, in Arabia, and Syria, and we can easily understand that in all these attacks Judæa, the natural sallying-port from Asia into Africa, and the natural point of union between Syria and Egypt, was sucked into the raging whirlpool and suffered severely.

Such a state of affairs was not calculated to recommend the reform of the prophets. On the contrary, the religious sentiment of the people could not but see in it all a punishment inflicted by the national Deity for the neglect of his wonted service. The popular religion understood the great danger that threatened it. The prophecies had smitten it with a deadly stroke, but it was nevertheless not inclined to give up the struggle without a blow. It accepted the challenge and soon wrested a victory from the reformers.

It is true, so long as Hezekiah lived, submission was imperative. For the reform had become a law of the kingdom, enacted by him, and was in a certain measure his personal creation. He died in the year 686, leaving the kingdom to Manasseh, his son, a child twelve years old. How it came to pass, will forever remain an enigma, owing to the utter lack of records; but the fact remains certain that under Manasseh a terrible and bloody reaction set in against the prophets. This is the period of which Jeremiah says that the sacred sword devoured the prophets like a raging lion, when all Jerusalem was full of innocent blood from one end to the other. All that Hezekiah had destroyed was restored. No memories of the hated innovations were suffered to remain.

A further step was taken. Genuine paganism now made its entry into Judæa and Jerusalem. The overpowering strength of the Assyrians must have made a deep impression on their contemporaries. Were not the gods of Assyria more mighty than the gods of the nations subjugated by it? And so we find under Manasseh the Assyrio-Babylonian worship of the stars introduced into Judæa, and solemn festivals held in honor of it in the temple at Jerusalem. Even foreign habits and customs were adopted. The healthful simplicity of the fathers was discarded to exchange therefor the dangerous blessings of an overrefined and vitiated civilisation. This also had its effect on the worship of God. The ritual became more and more gaudy and elaborate. Incense, of which ancient Israel knew nothing, appears from this time as an essential constituent of the service, and even that most terrible of religious aberrations, the sacrificing of children, fully calculated to excite with gruesome and voluptuous titillation the unstrung nerves of an overwrought civilisation, became the fashion. King Manasseh himself made his firstborn son pass through the fire, and everywhere in Jerusalem did the altars of Moloch send up their smoke, whilst a bloody persecution was instituted against the prophets and all their party.

These events made on the minds of the devout men in Israel an indelible impression, and the prophecies of Isaiah as to the indestructibility of Zion and of the House of David, were forgotten in their terror. It became the settled conviction of the best spirits that God could never forgive all this, but that, owing to the sins of Manasseh, the destruction both of Judah and Jerusalem was inevitable.

It is a memorable fact that during this whole period, almost, prophecy remained dumb in Israel. We can only point to one brief fragment with anything like assurance, and that is now read as Chapter 6 and the beginning of Chapter 7 of the book of Micah. This fragment is one of the most beautiful that we possess, and still resounds, borne on Palestrina's magic notes, as an improperia, on every Good Friday in the Sistine Chapel at Rome. God pleads with Israel:

"O, my people, what have I done unto thee? And wherein have I wearied thee? Testify against me."

And as now the people bow themselves down before God in answer to His divine accusations, and are anxious to give up everything, even the first-born, for their transgressions, then speaks the prophet:

"He hath shewed thee, O man, what is good; and what doth the Lord require of thee, but to do justly, and to love mercy, and to walk humbly with thy God?"

This fragment is important, as testifying how during this time of heavy affliction and persecution, piety deepened and became more spiritual; how it retired within itself and saw itself in an ever truer and clearer light, finally to come forth purified and strengthened.

Prophecy was again aroused from its slumbers by the trumpet notes of the world's history. In 650 the Assyrian empire was, if anything, greater and mightier than ever. But now destiny knocked at its gates. From the coasts of the Black Sea a storm broke forth over Asia, such as man had never before witnessed. Wild tribes of horsemen, after the manner of the later Huns and Mongolians, overran for more than twenty years all Asia on their fast horses, which seemed never to tire, spreading everywhere desolation and terror. Egypt had torn itself away from the rule of the Assyrians, and a new and terrible enemy in the Medes who were now consolidating their forces in the rear of Nineveh appeared. The Assyrian world-edifice cracked in all its joints, and grave revolutions were imminent. At once prophecy is at hand with the small but exceedingly valuable book of Zephaniah. The thunder of the last judgment rolls in Zephaniah's powerful words, whose dithyrambic lilt and wondrous music no translation can render. The *Dies iræ, dies illa*, which the Roman Church and the whole musical world now sings as a requiem, is taken word for word from Zephaniah.

"The great day of the Lord is near, it is near and hasteth greatly, even the voice of the day of the Lord; the mighty man shall cry there bitterly. That day is a day of wrath, a day of trouble and distress, a day of wasteness and desolation, a day of darkness and gloominess, a day of clouds and thick darkness. A day of the trumpet and alarm against the fenced cities and against the high towers. And I will bring distress upon men, that they shall walk like blind men because they have sinned against the Lord; and their blood shall be poured out as dust, and their marrow as the dung. Neither their silver nor their gold shall be able to deliver them in the day of the Lord's wrath; but the whole land shall be devoured by the fire of his jealousy: for he shall make even a speedy riddance of all them that dwell in the land."

The cause of this terrible judgment is the sins of Manasseh, which Zephaniah describes with drastic vividness at the beginning of his book. Only the righteous and the meek of the earth shall escape, who will form at the end of time a people pleasing unto God.

In the time of Nahum events had progressed still further. His book has for its sole subject the impending destruction of Nineveh. It was probably written in the year 625, as the Medes under king Phraortes made their first attack on Nineveh, but did not accomplish their aim. The merited judgment shall now fall upon the Assyrian nation for all the oppressions and persecutions which it has brought upon the world, and especially on the land and people of God. In a religious and prophetic sense the contents of the book are not important, but its æsthetic and poetical value is on that account the higher, the language full of power and strength, and possessing a pathos and fervor which only true passion can inspire. It is in a certain measure the cry of distress and revenge from all the nations oppressed and downtrodden by that detestable people, which is here re-echoed to us with irresistible power from the Book of Nahum.

The Book of Habakkuk also belongs to this series. The destruction of Nineveh is its subject. But in Habakkuk's Book the Chaldeans appear as the future instruments of the divine wrath. Habakkuk is a master of eloquence and imagery. His description of the Assyrian as the robber who opens his jaws like hell, and is as insatiable as death, who devoureth all people, and swalloweth down all nations, is among the most magnificent productions of Hebrew literature.

"He treateth men as the fishes of the sea, as creeping things that have no ruler over them. He fishes up all of them with the angle, he catches them in his net, and gathers them in his drag; therefore does he rejoice and is glad. Therefore he sacrifices unto his net, and burns incense unto his drag, because by them is his portion plenteous and his meat fat. Shall he then ever draw his sword, and not spare continually to slay the nations?"

In Habakkuk the ethical and religious element is duly treated. Pride causes the fall of the Assyrian, the *hybris* in the sense of Greek tragedy, for, as Habakkuk sharply and clearly expresses it, he makes "his strength his God." Might for the Assyrian exceeds right. Because he has the might, he oppresses and enslaves nations which have done him no harm. The universal moral law demands his destruction.

* * *

But now we must retrace our steps for a time. As Zephaniah, Nahum, and Habakkuk form an intimately connected group, it appeared expedient to treat them together. But Jeremiah appeared before Nahum, and between Nahum and Habakkuk an event happened which ranks among the most important and momentous in the history of mankind.

DEUTERONOMY.

UNDER King Manasseh the ancient popular religion had won a complete and bloody victory over the prophets. But, like all spiritual powers, prophecy could only gain by being combated and persecuted. The blood of its martyrs had not flowed in vain, and new life was soon to spring from it.

In 641 B. C., King Manasseh died and was succeeded by Amon, his son. During the latter's life, things continued as they were. In the second year of his reign, however, Amon was murdered in his own house by his servants. The Book of Kings recounts this event, but tells us nothing of the accompanying circumstances, and nothing at all of the cause of the conspiracy. The book, continuing, says, that the people slew the conspirators and placed Josiah, the son of the murdered king, a boy of eight, on the throne.

If ever we had just ground for complaint, it exists here. We know really nothing of this extraordinarily important century, except a few scattered facts. The great main-springs of its action are entirely hidden from us, and the results only are known. From a youth of Josiah's age naturally nothing was to be expected. The government was in the hands of corrupt courtiers, the people as described by Zephaniah worshipped both the God of Israel and Baal, Moloch and the hosts of heaven, that is the stars, clad themselves after strange fashions, and filled the house of the Lord with violence and deceit,—who were settled on their lees and who spake in their hearts, "The Lord does no good, neither evil!"

But the times were such as to rouse even these careless spirits. Men were gradually coming to see the gravity of the situation, and slowly but surely an inner change seems to have been wrought in the hearts of the people. The prophetic party, which had apparently not been persecuted for some time, must have kept up secretly a continuous and successful agitation. The priests in the temple of Jerusalem must have been won over to it, or at least influenced by it, and especially must its aspirations have found access to the heart of the young king, who, from all we know of him, was a thoroughly good and noble character.

The time now appeared ripe for a bold stroke.

When, in the eighteenth year of Josiah, 621 B.C., Shaphan the scribe paid an official visit to the temple of Jerusalem, the priest Hilkiah handed to him a book of laws which had been found there. Shaphan took the book and immediately brought it to the King, before whom he read it.

The impression which the book made on the King must have been tremendous. He rent his garments, and sent at once a deputation to Huldah, the prophetess, who was the wife of one of his privy officers and evidently held in high esteem. Huldah declared in favor of the book, and the King now went energetically to work. The entire people were convened in the temple at Jerusalem, and the King entered with them into a covenant. Both parties mutually and solemnly pledged themselves to acknowledge this book as the fundamental law of the kingdom, and to observe its commands. Upon the basis of it, a thorough reorganisation was effected and the celebrated reform of worship carried out, of which we read in the Book of Kings.

The events of the year 621 at Jerusalem were apparently of no great moment. But their consequences have been simply immeasurable. By them Israel, nay, the whole world, has been directed into new courses. We are to-day still under the influence of beliefs which were then promulgated for the first time, under the sway of forces which then first came into life. It is imperative, therefore, to enter into this matter more minutely, as the entire later development of prophecy is quite unintelligible unless we have a clear conception of it.

Our first question must be: What is this book of laws of Josiah, which was discovered in the year 621? The youthful De Wette, in his thesis for a professorship at Jena in the year 1805, clearly proved that this book of laws was essentially the fifth book of Moses, known as Deuteronomy. The book is clearly and distinctly marked off from the rest of the Pentateuch and its legislation, whilst the reforms of worship introduced by Josiah correspond exactly to what it called for. The proofs adduced by De Wette have been generally accepted, and his view has become a common possession of Old Testament research, having afforded us our first purchase, so to speak, for a true understanding of the religious history of Israel.

The conceptions and aims of Deuteronomy are thoroughly prophetic. It seeks to realise the hoped for Kingdom of God as promised by the prophets. Israel is to become a holy people, governed by the will of God; and this holiness is to be manifested through worship and justice, so that man shall serve God righteously and judge his fellow-men uprightly. The first point is the more important with Deuteronomy; its chief attention is devoted to the cultus, and here it broke away, in all fundamental points, from the ideas of ancient Israel and turned the development of things into entirely new courses.

The fundamental problem of religion is the relation between God and the world. Ancient Israel had seen both in one; all things worldly appeared to it divine; in everything appertaining to the world it found the expressions and revelations of God. The entire national life was governed and ruled by religion; in all places and all things God was to his people a living and real presence. The result of this naturally was the secularisation of God, which the prophets felt to be an exceedingly grave danger. The right solution of the problem would have been that given by Jesus, who openly recognised the divinisation of the world as the rightful task of religion—to fill and sanctify the world with the spirit of God, and thus to make it a place and a field for God's work, a Kingdom of God, and a temple of the Holy Spirit. Deuteronomy pursues a different course; it dissolves the bond between God and the world, tears them asunder, and ends by depriving the world entirely of its divinity. On the one hand, a world without a God; on the other, a God without a world. Nevertheless, this last was more the result than the intention of Deuteronomy. At least, wherever it consciously carries out this view it is justified, especially when it requires that God shall not be worshipped through symbols or images, and that every figurative representation of the Godhead, or its simulation by certain venerated forms of nature, must be destroyed root and branch. We have here merely the outcome of the prophetic apprehension that God is a spirit, and therefore must be worshipped as a spirit. But Deuteronomy makes additional requirements. Obviously in consequence of the dogma of Isaiah respecting the central importance of Mount Zion as the dwelling-place of God on earth, Deuteronomy insists that God can only be worshipped at Jerusalem; only there should acts of adoration be permitted, and all other sanctuaries and places of worship outside of Jerusalem should be destroyed.

The idea that the centralisation of worship in a single place rendered it easier of supervision and ensured the preservation of its purity may have contributed to the adoption of this last measure; and it must certainly be admitted that the local sanctuaries in smaller towns were really breeding-places of flagrant abuses. But the consequences of the measure were simply incalculable. It was virtually tantamount to a suppression of religion in the whole country outside of Jerusalem.

Up to this time, every town and village had had its sanctuary, and access to God was an easy matter for every Israelite. When his heart moved him either to give expression to his thanks, or to seek consolation in his sorrow, he had only to go to his place of worship. Every difficult question of law was laid before God; that is, argued in the sanctuary and decided by a solemn oath of purification. And to one and all these sanctuaries granted the right of refuge. Here was the fugitive safe from his pursuer, and he could only be removed from the sanctuary and delivered up provided he were a convicted felon. Moreover, in the old days of Israel all these sanctuaries were oracles, where at any time men could ask advice or aid in difficult or dangerous matters. And many things which have for us a purely secular character, were to the ancient Israelites acts of divine service. Every animal slaughtered was a sacrifice; every indulgence in meat, a sacrificial feast.

All this ceased with the legislation of Deuteronomy. The Israelite was now compelled to carry on his daily life without God, and thus accustomed himself to consider life as something apart from religion, and in no wise connected with God. Religion was reduced to the three great feasts, which Deuteronomy likewise fundamentally reconstituted.

In ancient Israel the three great feasts were thanksgiving festivals. At the feast of the unleavened bread the first fruits of the fields, of the barley harvest, were offered up to God. The Feast of Weeks, or Pentecost, was the regular harvest feast, when the wheat was garnered, and the Feast of Tabernacles was the autumn festival, the feast of the ingathering of the wine and the fruit. This natural foundation of the three great festivals, which brought them into organic relation with each individual and his personal life, and in fact formed for him the real crises of his life, was now destroyed, and an ecclesiastical or ecclesiastico-historical basis given to them. The feast of unleavened bread took place in remembrance of the flight out of Egypt; the Feast of Weeks later in remembrance of the giving of the law on Sinai, the Feast of Tabernacles in remembrance of the journey through the desert, when Israel dwelt in tents. A difference thus was created spontaneously between holy events and secular events, week days and festivals. Routine every-day life was secularised, while religion was made into an institution, ordinance, work, and achievement apart by itself.

A further outcome of Deuteronomy was, that a distinct and rigorously exclusive priesthood now appears as the sole lawful ministers and stewards of the cultus, and it was enacted that all its members should be descended from the tribe of Levi. In olden times the father of the family offered up the sacrifices for himself and household; he was the priest of his house. To be sure, larger sanctuaries and professional priests were already in existence, but the people were not restricted to them. Every house was still a temple of God, and every head of a family a priest of the Most High. Deuteronomy did away with all this, and so first created the distinction between clergy and laity. Man, as such, has nothing to do directly with God, but only a privileged class of men possess this prerogative and right.

In this way Deuteronomy also radically transformed the priesthood. In ancient Israel the priest was primarily the minister of the divine oracle, the interpreter and expositor of the Divine Will. Deuteronomy did away with oracular predictions as heathenish, and converted the priest into a sacrificer and expounder of the law. The character of the sacrifice also was completely altered. The Israelite now only offered up sacrifices at the three great yearly festivals, when he was compelled to be in Jerusalem. He could hardly be expected to undertake a journey to Jerusalem merely for the sake of making a thanksgiving offering. There was, however, a species of sacrifice which allowed of no delay,—the sacrifice of sin and atonement. Here, in restoring man's broken relations with God, no time could be lost. Accordingly, the sin and atonement offerings now assume increasing dominance; the whole cultus becomes more and more an institution for the propitiation of sins, and the priest, the intermediator who negotiates the forgiveness.

Still another consequence flowed from the ideas of Deuteronomy—the opposition of Church and State. This also Deuteronomy created. If the whole of human life has in itself something profane, and the religious life is restricted to a definite caste, man is, so to speak, torn into two halves, each of which lives its own life. In ancient Israel man saw a divine dispensation in the public and national life; love of country was a religious duty. The king was the chief high priest of the people; all State acts were sanctified through religion, and when men fought for home and country, they fought for God "the fight of God." But now all that was changed. The State as such had nothing more to do with the religious life, and we even see the beginnings in Deuteronomy of that development which subsequently set the Church over the State and regarded the latter merely as the handmaid of the former. Civil State life became a matter of ecclesiastical cult. This, in a sense, was providential. By the separation of religion from the State, the religion of

Israel was enabled to survive the destruction of the Jewish State which followed thirty-five years later. But its ultimate consequences were direful beyond measure.

Nor was this all that Deuteronomy did. It substituted for the living revelation of God in the human heart and in history, the dead letter. For the first time a book was made the foundation of religion, religion a statute, a law. He who followed what was written in this book was religious, and he alone.

We see, thus, how an indubitable deepening of the religious spirit is followed by a fixed externalism, and how the prophetic assumptions led to thoroughly unprophetic conclusions. Deuteronomy is an attempt to realise the prophetic ideas by external means. This naturally brought in its train the externalisation of those ideas. In Deuteronomy prophecy gained a decided victory over the national religion, but it was largely a Pyrrhic victory. Prophecy abdicated in favor of priesthood. It is worthy of note that Deuteronomy makes provision for the event of a prophet appearing who might teach doctrines not written in this holy book, of which the priests are the natural guardians and interpreters. As in earlier times the monarchy and prophecy were the two dominant powers, so now priesthood and the law ruled supreme.

But Deuteronomy was productive of still other results. The opposition of secular and sacred, of laity and clergy, of State and Church, the conception of a holy writ and of a divine inspiration, can be traced back in its last roots to the Deuteronomy of the year 621, together with the whole history of revealed religion down to the present time, including not only Judaism but Christianity and Islam, who have simply borrowed these ideas from Judaism.

By whom this book, which is perhaps the most significant and most momentous that was ever written, was composed, we do not know. It represents a compromise between prophecy and priesthood, and might therefore have been compiled by the priests of Jerusalem, as indeed it was a priest who delivered it to the king, and the priests who derived all the benefits from it. It may be regarded as pretty certain that it took its origin in this period.

Josiah regarded the demands of this book with reverent awe. We are not told whether his reforms were opposed by the people, although he carried them out with great severity and harshness. The final establishment of regularity must have been looked upon as a blessing, and the more so as Deuteronomy lays particular stress on civil justice, establishing in this domain also stability and order. Moreover, Josiah was a man who by his personal qualities was fitted to render acceptable the oppressive features of the work, and to win for it able partisans.

JEREMIAH.

PROPHECY did not experience at once the disastrous consequences of the priestly reforms of 621, but displayed at this period its noblest offshoot in Jeremiah. It is impossible to suppose that Jeremiah had anything to do with either the composition or introduction of Deuteronomy. The rather elaborate account given of the proceedings of this period in the Book of Kings makes no mention of him, and the mental relationship which some have claimed to exist between Jeremiah and Deuteronomy is based on passages of this book which did not belong to the law-code of 621, but are later than Jeremiah, and the direct outcome of his influence.

As the Kingdom of Israel on its downfall bore in Hosea its noblest prophetic fruit, so in the time immediately preceding the destruction of Judah we find the sublime figure of Jeremiah. Mentally, also, these two men were closely related. Sentiment is the predominant characteristic of each. Both have the same tender and sympathetic heart; both have the same elegiac bent of mind; both were pre-eminently devout men. The religious element preponderates entirely over the ethical. It can be proved that Jeremiah was powerfully influenced by Hosea, and that he looked upon him as his prototype.

We are better informed concerning the life and fortunes of Jeremiah than of any other prophet. He received his call to the prophetic office in the thirteenth year of Josiah's reign, namely, in 627. He must have been at the time very young, as he hesitated to obey the divine order on the ground of his youth. We are referred, therefore, to the later years of the reign of King Manasseh, as the period of the prophet's birth. Jeremiah was not a native of Jerusalem; his home was Anathoth, a small village near Jerusalem. He came of a priestly family, and we get the impression that he did not live in poor circumstances. Solomon had banished to his estate in Anathoth, Abiathar, the high-priest of David, and the last remaining heir of the old priesthood of Shiloh. The conjecture is not rash, perhaps, that Jeremiah was a descendant of this family, which could cherish and preserve the proudest and dearest recollections of Israel as its family traditions. The family was descended from Moses. Abiathar had been closely attached to David's person and throne; he had given the religious sanction to all David's mighty deeds, and it was he who helped to found Jerusalem as also to be the first to worship there the God of Israel. How vividly such traditions are wont to be fostered in fallen families is well known. Further than that, Jeremiah shows himself to be thoroughly acquainted with the past history of Israel. Moses and Samuel, Amos and Hosea,—such were the men with whom and in whom he lived. No other prophet is so steeped in the ancient literature and history of Israel. Everything that was noble and worthy in Israel was known and familiar to him. We see in this the fruits of a careful education, and can readily imagine how the priestly father or pious mother filled the impressionable heart of the child with what was most sacred to them.

Jeremiah himself mentions his debt to his parents, where God says to him in the vision: "Before thou camest forth out of the womb I sanctified and ordained thee a prophet." Which means: A person born of such parents must of necessity be consecrated to God.

And still another circumstance is of utmost importance. Jeremiah is the scion of a martyred church. He was born at a time when Manasseh persecuted the prophets with fire and sword, and raged against their whole party. Persecution, however, only serves to fan religion into a more intense flame. With what fervor do men then pray; with what strength do they believe and confide, wait and hope. Under such circumstances was Jeremiah born. Under such impressions he grew up. Truly, he was a predestined personality.

In Jeremiah prophecy appears in a totally distinctive character, noticeable even in his first calling in the year 627. God says to Jeremiah: "See I have this day set thee over the nations and over the kingdoms, to root out and to pull down, to build and to plant." So thoroughly does the prophet feel himself one with Him who sent him, and conceive his own personality absorbed in God! Likewise, in one of the grandest passages of his book it is he who causes all the nations to drink of the wine-cup of God's fury. And thus the whole life of the prophet is bound up in his calling. He must even deny himself the joys of matrimony and of home. Solitary and forlorn he must wander through life, belonging only to God and to his vocation.

It is my duty to state, so as not to draw on myself the charge of false embellishment, that this consciousness of absolute union with God often assumes in Jeremiah a form which has for us something offensive in it. His enemies are also God's enemies, and this otherwise tender and gentle man calls down upon them the heaviest curses: "Pull them out like sheep for the slaughter, and prepare them for the day of throttling." But he is conscious himself that this is something incongruous. In one of his most remarkable passages, where he has broken out into the direst imprecations and cursed himself and the day of his birth, God answers him: "If thou becomest again mine, thou mayest again be my servant, and if thou freest thy better self from the vile, then shalt thou still be as my mouth."

Jeremiah did indeed free his better self from the

vile, and such passing outbreaks only make him dearer to us and render him more human, as showing us what this man inwardly suffered, how he struggled, and under what afflictions his prophecy arose. The sorrow he bears is twofold: personal, in that he preaches to deaf ears and only reaps hate in return for his love; and general, as a member of his people. For as the prophet knows himself to be in his vocation one with God, so does he know himself as a man to be one with his people, whose grief he bears with a double burden, whose destiny is like to break his heart.

"My bowels, my bowels, I am pained to my very heart; my heart maketh a noise in me; I cannot hold my peace, because thou hast heard, O my soul, the sound of the trumpet, the alarm of war."

Thus he exclaims in one place, and in another we read:

"O that my head were waters, and my eyes a fountain of tears, that I might weep day and night for the slain of the daughter of my people!"

Out of this peculiar and twofold position of the prophet between God and his people Jeremiah drew the practical inference that he was the chosen advocate and intercessor of the nation with God; in his ardent prayers he fairly battles with God for the salvation of his people. This is a totally new feature. The relation of the former prophets to their contemporaries was that of mere preachers of punishment and repentance. Jeremiah, however, in spite of their unworthiness, holds his fellow-countrymen lovingly in his heart and endeavors to arrest the arm of God, already uplifted to deal on them the destructive blow. God at last must all but rebuff his unwearying and impetuous prophet.

The prophetic preaching of Jeremiah naturally often rests on that of his predecessors, out of which it organically grew. But it is curious to see, and this is noticeable even in the smallest details, how everything is spiritualised and deepened in Jeremiah, and in a certain measure transposed to a higher key. Often it is a mere descriptive word, or characteristic expression, which makes old thoughts appear new, and stamps them as the mental property of Jeremiah. I must forego the proof of this in detail, and limit myself in this brief sketch to what is specifically new in Jeremiah, and to what constitutes his substantial importance and position in the history of Israelitic prophecy and religion.

Now, the specifically new in Jeremiah touches directly the kernel and substance of religion. Jeremiah was the first to set religion consciously free from all extraneous and material elements, and to establish it on a purely spiritual basis. God himself will destroy His temple in Jerusalem, and at the time of the final salvation, it shall not be built up again, and the Holiest of Holies, the ark of the covenant, will not be missed, and none new made. What God requires of man is something different: man shall break up his fallow ground and not sow among thorns; he shall circumcise his heart. God considers only the purity of the heart, its prevalent disposition; it is he who "tries the heart and the reins"—an expression originally coined by Jeremiah, and which we meet with in his book for the first time. Truth and obedience are good in themselves, as denoting a moral disposition.

There was a sect, the Rechabites, who abstained from drinking wine. Jeremiah knew well that the Kingdom of God was not eating and drinking, and that the goodness and worth of man in God's sight did not depend on whether he drank wine or not. Nevertheless, he praises these Rechabites, and holds them up to the people as an example of piety and faith. Jeremiah indeed goes further than this. He is the first to affirm in clear and plain words, that the gods of the heathen are not real beings, but merely imaginative creations in the minds of their worshippers. Yet he holds up to his people the heathen who serve their false and meaningless religion with genuine faith and sincere devotion, as models and examples which put them to shame. They are really more pleasing to God than a people who have the true God, but are unmindful and forgetful of Him. And this is a sin for which there is no excuse, for the knowledge of God is inborn in man. As the bird of passage knoweth the time of his departure and the object of his wandering, so is the longing for God born in man; he has only to follow after that yearning of his heart as the animal after its instinct, and this craving must lead him to God. And this will also be in the final time when God concludes a new covenant with Israel: then has every man the law of God written in his heart; he has only to consult his heart and to follow after its directions. Now, if religion, or, as Jeremiah calls it, the knowledge of God, is born in man, then there is no difference between Jews and Gentiles, and this grand thought Jeremiah first recognised:

"O Lord, . . . the Gentiles shall come unto thee from the ends of the earth and shall say, Our fathers have inherited only lies, vanity, and things wherein there is no profit. Can a man make gods unto himself, that are not gods?" And when the Gentiles then learn from converted Israel to worship the true God, as they themselves taught Israel to offer sacrifices to idols, then they, too, will enter into the future kingdom of God.

The ideality and universality of religion—these are the two new grand apprehensions which Jeremiah has given to the world. Every man as such is born a child of God. He does not become such through the forms of any definite religion, or outward organisation, but he becomes such in his heart, through circumcision of the heart and of the ears. A pure heart and a pure mind are all that God requires of man, let his piety choose what form it will, so long as it is genuine. Thus we have in Jeremiah the purest and highest consummation of the prophecy of Israel and of the religion of the Old Testament. After him One only could come, who was greater than he.

But we must now pass on to a consideration of the life and fortunes of Jeremiah, for in them are reflected the fortunes of his people and age.

In the early days of his vocation as a prophet, Jeremiah seems to have worked very quietly. For the first five years, during the occurrence of the extremely important events enacted at Jerusalem in connexion with Deuteronomy, nobody took the slightest notice of him. Perhaps he was still living in his native village of Anathoth. We know from his own accounts that he labored there, as also that he was the object of a rancorous persecution, which aimed at his life. It is possible that it was this that induced him to settle in Jerusalem.

Of his work during the reign of Josiah we know nothing definite. Only one short speech of the collection in his book is expressly ascribed to this time. In fact, we are told nothing of Josiah himself, after the famous reform, except the manner of his death. The second half of his reign must have been on the whole happy and propitious for Judah. The Scythian storm had raged across it without causing much severe damage. The power of Assyria was smitten and had entirely disappeared in the outlying regions. Josiah could rule over Israel as if it were his own land, and in a measure restore the kingdom of David.

But events pursued their uninterruptible course.

In the year 608 Nineveh was surrounded by the allied Medes and Chaldeans, and its fall was only a question of time. The Egyptian Pharaoh Necho held this to be a fitting opportunity to secure for himself his portion of the heritage of Assyria. He set forth with a huge army from the Nile, to occupy on behalf of the Egyptian kingdom the whole country up to the Euphrates. What moved Josiah to oppose him we do not know. A disastrous engagement took place at Megiddo, where Josiah was completely defeated and mortally wounded. This was for the religious party in Israel a terrible blow. Josiah, the first king pleasing to God, had met a dreadful end. He had served God faithfully and honestly, and now God had abandoned him. Could not some mistake have been made as to God's power, or as to His justice? And indeed after this event a change does really seem to have taken place in the religious views.

Jehoiakim, Josiah's eldest son, who now ruled as an Egyptian vassal, was not a man after the heart of the prophet; in him Manasseh lived anew. He also persecuted the prophets. He ordered one of them named Urijah to be executed, and Jeremiah himself was in constant danger of losing his life. Whether the reform of the cultus ordered by Josiah was revoked, we do not know; in any event Jekoiakim took no interest in it, and in no wise supported it. Under him the temporal arm of the church was not available. And now, just at the beginning of his reign, Jeremiah appears with the awful prophecy, at that time doubly monstrous and blasphemous, that temple and city would both be destroyed if a radical improvement and thorough conversion did not take place. Violent scenes arose in the temple; the death of the obnoxious prophet was clamorously called for. He was saved only with difficulty, and it seems was forbidden to enter the temple and to preach there.

In the year 606 Nineveh fell after a three years' siege, and thus disappeared the kingdom and nation of the Assyrians from the face of the earth. The Medes and Chaldeans divided the spoils among them. Now, however, they had another task on their hands. A third competitor was to be driven out of the field. Pharaoh Necho had actually occupied the whole country up to the Euphrates. Accordingly, in 605, a year after the fall of Nineveh, the Babylonian Nebuchadnezzar marched against him. The battle took place at Carchemish and Necho was totally defeated. The Egyptian hosts rolled back in wild flight to their homes and the whole country as far as the confines of Egypt fell into Nebuchadnezzar's hands.

In this critical year, 605, Jeremiah received God's command to write down in a book all the words which he had hitherto spoken, and at the end of the book we find the vision of the cup of wrath, which the prophet was to cause all nations and peoples to drink, for now through the Chaldeans God's judgment is fulfilled over the whole earth. Jehoiakim felt the seriousness of the situation. A general fast was ordered, and seizing the occasion Jeremiah caused his young friend and pupil Baruch to read his book of prophecies aloud in the temple. The King heard of it, ordered the book to be read to him, had it cut into pieces and cast into the fire. He ordered the arrest of Jeremiah and Baruch, but they managed to keep out of the way.

Thus Jehoiakim was converted from an Assyrian into a Babylonian vassal; and Jeremiah incessantly urged upon him the necessity of bending his neck to the yoke of the King of Babel. For Nebuchadnezzar was the servant, the chosen weapon of God, appointed by Him to rule over the earth. Natural prudence and insight alone would have recommended this policy as the only right and possible one; for by it relative quiet and peace were assured to the nation. But Jehoiakim did not think so. He arose against the King of Babel, and a storm now brewed around Jerusalem. Jehoiakim himself did not survive the catastrophe, but his son Jehoiachin was compelled to surrender unconditionally to the Babylonians. Nebuchadnezzar led the king captive to Babylon, where he was kept in close bondage, together with ten thousand of his people, the entire aristocracy of birth and intellect; nothing remained but the lower classes. He set the third son of Josiah, Zedekiah, as vassal king over this decimated and enfeebled people.

All this happened in the year 597.

Better days now began for Jeremiah. Zedekiah

resembled his father Josiah; he evidently held the prophet in high esteem, and seemed not indisposed to be guided by him. But he had to reckon here with the wishes of the people and with public opinion, and they tended the other way. The sadder the situation and the more dangerous the circumstances became, the higher flared the fanaticism, which was fanned into a flame by other prophets. Here we encounter those biassed and undiscriminating disciples of Isaiah, who, with their boasts of the indestructibility of Jerusalem and the temple, were never weary of assuring the people of divine protection, and of urging them to shake off the detested yoke of the Gentiles.

In the fourth year of the reign of Zedekiah a powerful and widespread agitation seems to have broken out. Ambassadors from all the smaller nations and peoples round about gathered in Jerusalem to plan some scheme of concerted action against Nebuchadnezzar. Jeremiah appears in their midst with a yoke around his neck. It is the will of God that all the nations should bow their necks beneath the yoke of Nebuchadnezzar, lest a heavier judgment should fall upon them. One of the false prophets, Hananiah, took the yoke from off the neck of Jeremiah and broke it, saying: "Even so will the Lord break the yoke of Nebuchadnezzar king of Babylon from the neck of all the nations within the space of two full years." Then said Jeremiah to him: "Thou hast broken the yokes of wood; but in their stead shall come yokes of iron."

It was predicted Hananiah should die in that year, for having prophesied falsely in the name of God. And Hananiah died in the seventh month. Finally, nothing definite came of the deliberations, and the nations remained quiet. But even the exiles in Babylon, who were also greatly excited and stirred up by false prophets, had to be warned by Jeremiah to peace and resignation in the will of God. He did this in a letter, which must have been written at the same time with the events above-mentioned.

Of the next five years we know nothing. But adversity takes rapid strides, and now the destiny of Jerusalem was about to be fulfilled. Confiding in the help of Egypt, Zedekiah rebelled against his suzerain and for a second time the Babylonian armies marched against Jerusalem. Zedekiah sent to consult the prophet as to the future. Jeremiah remained firm in his opinion—subjection to the King of Babylon. Whosoever shall go forth against the Chaldeans shall not escape out of their hands, and whosoever shall remain in the city shall die through the sword, hunger, and pestilence, but the city shall be consumed with fire. The people did not listen to him; passion had blinded and rendered them foolish. The siege began. The Egyptians, however, kept their promise. Egyptian troops poured in, and Nebuchadnezzar raised the siege.

The joy in Jerusalem knew no bounds. But unfortunately these days of rejoicing and confidence were darkened by a disgraceful breach of faith. The necessities of the siege had suggested the revival of an ancient custom, by which the Hebrew slaves were set free after six years' service. To obtain warriors willing to fight during the siege, the Hebrew slaves had been solemnly liberated, but now that all danger was over, they were compelled to return to servitude. The enraged prophet hurled his most terrible words at the heads of this faithless and perjured people, but in so doing he made enemies among the ruling classes, who, as he was about to set forth to his birthplace Anathoth, caused him to be arrested, on the pretence that he intended to go over to the Chaldeans; he was beaten and put into prison. But his prophecy was right. The Chaldeans returned, and the siege began anew. That was for Jeremiah a time of affliction. Hated, ill-treated, persecuted by all as a betrayer of his country, he passed several weeks and months of unutterable misery. To the energetic mediation of King Zedekiah he owed his life.

We can now understand, perhaps, the moods which caused him to curse his birth and to murmur against God, who had only suffered him to be born for misery and wretchedness, hatred and enmity.

But soon the fate of Jerusalem was fulfilled. After being defended with the wild courage of despair, it was finally captured on the ninth of July, 586. This time Nebuchadnezzar showed no mercy. Zedekiah had his eyes put out and was carried in chains to Babylon, after all his children had been murdered in his sight. The city and temple were plundered, burnt with fire, and utterly destroyed, and almost the entire population carried away captive into Babylon. Only a few of the poor of the land were left behind for vine-dressers and for husbandmen. As Babylonian viceroy over this miserable remnant, with a residence in Mizpah, was appointed Gedaliah, a grandson of Shaphan, the scribe who had delivered Deuteronomy to King Josiah.

Jeremiah, who had survived all the terrors and sufferings of the siege and capture, and whom the Chaldeans had left in Judah, remained with Gedaliah, whose father, Ahikam had been a warm friend and supporter of the prophet. And now that his prophecies soared to their sublimest heights and he had just predicted on the ruins of Jerusalem and of the temple, God's everlasting covenant of grace with Israel, he would, perhaps, have still enjoyed a successful activity, had not a band of fanatics with a prince of the royal blood at their head, treacherously attacked and slain Gedaliah and such Chaldeans as were with him. Jeremiah still counselled quiet. Nebuchadnezzar would not visit the crime of a few on the whole nation. But the people would not trust him; they arose and went into Egypt and forced the aged prophet to accompany them.

In Egypt the prophet closed a life full of suffering. Bitter contentions arose with his countrymen. Jeremiah still fearlessly discharged his office as incarnate conscience of his people, and was, according to a Jewish tradition, stoned to death by an infuriated mob.

Thus, breathed out his great soul Jeremiah, solitary and alone on Egyptian soil under the blows of his own people, for whom during his whole lifetime he had striven and suffered, and from whom, for all his love and faith, he had but reaped hatred and persecution. Truly he drank the cup of suffering to its dregs. But undismayed and dauntless, he fell in his harness, a true soldier of the truth. He had become as an iron wall, and as pillars of brass against the whole land. They had struggled against him, but not overcome him. He fell as a hero, as a conqueror; he could die for the truth, he could not abjure it.

Jerusalem destroyed, its greatest son buried in the sands of Egypt, the people dragged as captives into Babylon—what was now to become of Israel? Here was the opportunity for Deuteronomy to prove itself true, and it did prove so. It saved Israel and religion. And to this end prophecy also helped much. If the songs of the Lord were silent in a strange land, and Israel weeping hung her harps on the willows by the waters of Babylon—yet prophecy was not silent. It found during the exile in Babylon two of its truest and spiritually most powerful exponents.

THE BABYLONIAN EXILE.

THE Assyrians were the first people to make use of the exile as a means of pacifying rebellious tribes. Whenever they chanced to come upon an especially hardy nationality, which offered determined opposition in its struggle for existence and was not willing to be swept away without resistance by the advancing avalanche, the entire nation was expelled from its land and dragged into the heart of the Assyrian empire, either directly into Assyria itself, or into regions which had been denationalised for generations and already been made Assyrian, whilst the depopulated country itself was filled with Assyrian colonists. The Assyrians had already noticed that the strong roots of the power of an individual as well as of a nation lie in its native soil. Home and country mutually determine each other and form an inseparable union. In those days they did so more than now, for then religion also was an integral part of the nation, and religion, too, was indissolubly associated with the soil. A nation's country was the home and dwelling-place of its national

Deity; to be torn away from one's native soil was equivalent to being torn away from Him, and thus was destroyed the strongest bond and the deepest source of nationality.

The object of the transportation was attained. Such members of the ten tribes of Israel as were carried away in the year 722 have disappeared without a trace, and if that branch of the Semites commonly known as the Aramaic has never exhibited a distinct ethnographical type in history, the fact may be ascribed to the five hundred years' dominion of the Assyrians in those regions, who from the earliest times systematically eradicated the national features of conquered countries.

In their national sentiments Israel did not differ from the other nations of antiquity. Every country except Palestine was unclean, and to hold there the service of God was impossible. For a man like the prophet Hosea, who did not suffer himself to be governed by prejudices, or allow his better judgment to be impaired, it was quite a matter of course that as soon as the people left the soil of Palestine, all service of God should cease of itself, and this for him is one of the deepest terrors of the threatened exile. He said:

"They shall not dwell in the Lord's land, but Ephraim shall return to Egypt and eat unclean things in Assyria. They shall not pour out wine-offerings to the Lord, neither shall they prepare burnt-offerings for Him; their bread shall be unto them as the bread of mourners; all that eat thereof shall be polluted: for their bread shall be for their appetite; it shall not come into the house of the Lord. What will ye do in the solemn day and in the day of the feast of the Lord?"

Such also was the thought one hundred and fifty years later, when Judah was carried into exile. The Babylonian government would have had no objection to the exiles building for themselves the altars and temples of their God in Mesopotamia—but it never entered the heads of the Jews to build a temple to God on the Euphrates, after that His own house on Mount Zion had been destroyed. Even the most religious man would have seen in this an insult, a mockery of the God of Israel: better not sacrifice at all than unclean things on unclean ground. And this condition of things was to last a long time. Jeremiah had distinctly named seventy years as the period during which God would grant dominion to the Chaldeans, and had repeatedly and urgently warned the exiles to make arrangements for a long sojourn in the strange land. How, now, did Israel pass this period of probation?

The consequences of the Babylonian exile have been momentous in every way; the exile in Babylon quite transformed Israel and its religion; it created what is known in religious history as Judaism, in contradistinction to Israelitism. To have been the first to clearly recognise that the Judaism of post-exilic times, although the organic outcome of the Israelitism of the exilic period, was yet something totally new and specifically different from it, is the great and imperishable service of De Wette, who was indeed the first to gain any understanding at all of the religious history of the Old Testament in its real significance and tendencies. That the exile into Babylon exercised this stupendous transformative influence, was the natural result of the circumstances and of the logic of facts.

A later writer of the Old Testament, whose name and period are unknown to us, he who gave to the Book of Amos the conciliatory conclusion already mentioned, compares the Babylonian captivity to a sieve, in which the house of Israel is sifted, through which all the chaff and dust passes, but not the least grain falls to the earth. This comparison is excellent and characterises the situation with a distinctness and sharpness that could not be improved upon.

The Babylonian exile did indeed bring about a separation of the religious from the irreligious section of the people, of the followers of the prophetic religion from the followers of the ancient popular religion. In the fall of Judah and the destruction of Jerusalem and the temple, the prophetic religion won a complete victory over the old religion of the people, and the latter lost every possibility of further existence. The ancient Deity of the nation vanished in the smoke sent up by the conflagration of the temple of Solomon. He was vanquished and destroyed by the gods of Nebuchadnezzar. His want of power had been plainly proved by the destruction of His people and of His house, and He himself lay buried beneath their ruins.

The moral influence of the Babylonian captivity and its attendant features must also be taken into account. Bowed down by the dread blows of fate, all confidence lost in themselves and their God, the Jews came, a despised and oppressed remnant, to Babylon, which was at that time in the zenith of its power and magnificence. What an overwhelming effect must the undreamt-of grandeur of their new surroundings have made upon them! Their once so loved and admired Jerusalem, how poor it must have appeared to them when compared with the metropolis of Babylon with its gigantic buildings, its art, its luxury! The temple of Solomon, at one time their pride and glory, was it not but a miserable village-church when likened to the wondrous edifice raised to the worship of the Babylonian God! As the great unknown writer towards the end of the captivity expresses it, Israel was here but a worm and Jacob a maggot. How irresistible the temptation must have been: "Away with the old trash, let us bow down and acknowledge this new and powerful deity!"

Moreover, it was a decided personal advantage for a Jew to renounce his nationality and to become a Babylonian. We have in the literary productions of the time woful complaints concerning the brutal mockery and heartless derision to which the poor Jews were subjected in exile, nay more, they were subject to ill-treatment and personal violence. An extraordinary strength of character was necessary to remain steadfast and true; only really earnest and convinced religious natures could resist such temptations. And thus the natural consequences of the conditions were that the half-hearted and lukewarm, the weak and those wanting in character, the worldly-minded, who thought only of personal advantage and honor, broke away, and that a refining process took place within Israel which left nothing remaining but the sacred remnant hoped for by Isaiah. Even on this remnant, which was really composed of the best and the noblest elements of the people, the Babylonian captivity had a profound effect. The religion of Israel, in fact, was destined to undergo a deep change.

Deuteronomy had already effected a separation between the State and the Church, between the national and the religious life. Of course, at the outset the reform had to reckon with these as concrete powers and weighty factors, but it is evident they stood in its way and formed serious obstacles to the realisation of its final aims, which were of a purely ecclesiastical character. But now destiny had removed these hindrances. The State was destroyed, the national life extirpated, nothing but the ecclesiastical element remained. The hard logic of facts itself had drawn the conclusions of Deuteronomy, and afforded them the freest play for their growth and operation. Judah as a nation was destroyed by the Babylonian captivity as completely as

Israel was by the Assyrian, but it was transformed into Judaism. The State became a Church; a nation was converted into a congregation. And this Judah, which had now become Judaism, had a world-wide mission to fulfil which was without parallel. The future and entire further development of religion depended upon it.

The first person who clearly recognised the situation of the Jews in the Babylonian captivity and sought to adapt the exiles to the change of conditions was Ezekiel, the son of Buzi. The significance and influence of this man cannot be rated too highly. He took the initiative step in the entire development which followed, and gave to it its theological foundations.

Ezekiel may be justly styled a theologian; he is the first dogmatist of the Old Testament.

EZEKIEL.

EZEKIEL was the son of a priest of the temple of Jerusalem, and had been carried off to Babylon with the first captives, under Jehoiachin, in the year 597. Five years later, 592, he appeared as prophet. His work lasted for twenty-two years, but we know nothing of its details. He was at first a mere herald of the judgment; the approaching complete destruction of Jerusalem was his only theme. But his companions in misery refused to listen to him. National fanaticism, blind confidence in God, who in the end must perforce aid both His people and His temple, had seized possession of their hearts. Derided and maligned, the prophet was forced to be silent, till the fulfilment of his threat by the destruction of Jerusalem loosed the seal from his mouth and from the ears and hearts of his people.

The Book of Ezekiel is the most voluminous of all the prophetic literature, and it is not easy to give in a few brief strokes a sketch of the man and of his importance, but I will try to emphasise at least the main points.

<u>Personality</u> is the characteristic of Ezekiel. Ezekiel was a man of a thoroughly practical nature with a wonderfully sharp perception of the problems and needs of his age; he understood how to read the signs of the times and to deduce the right lessons from them. In this respect he bears a most wonderful resemblance to Isaiah, with whom he has also a marked relationship of character. The key-note in the character of both is the immeasurable distance between God and man. In the image of God the predominant and decisive feature is His sanctity and majesty, His absolutely supramundane elevation in ethical and metaphysical matters, the consequence being that humility is the cardinal virtue of man. When confronting his God, Ezekiel feels himself to be only the "son of man." When thought worthy of a divine revelation, he falls on his face to the ground, and it is God who raises him up and sets him on his feet. He has, in common with Isaiah, the same terrible moral earnestness, a certain vein of severity and harshness, which does not suffer the tenderer tones of the heart to come into full play.

One of the most learned theologians of the present day has compared this prophet to Gregory VII. and Calvin, in both of whom personal amiability and sympathy are wanting, but who excite our unbounded admiration as men and characters by the iron consistency of their thought and the hard energy of their actions. There is much that is true and befitting in this comparison. Ezekiel—if I may be allowed the expression—is pre-eminently churchman and organiser; as such, the greatest that Israel ever had. He has left, in this respect, the imprint of his mind on all future ages, and marked out for them the path of development.

As Isaiah transformed into practice the ideas of Amos and Hosea, so Ezekiel is thoroughly dependent on his great predecessor Jeremiah. He drew the conclusions from the religious subjectivism and individualism of Jeremiah, and bestowed upon them the corrective which they urgently needed.

I will now endeavor to group together and to characterise the leading thoughts of Ezekiel in their most important aspects. The first thing Ezekiel is called upon to do is to vindicate God, even as against his most pious contemporaries.

"The way of the Lord is the wrong way," was a remark that Ezekiel must have repeatedly heard. And such views were not urged without a certain amount of justification. Were the people and the period just previous to the destruction of Jerusalem so especially wicked and godless? Had not King Josiah done everything to fulfil the demands of God? Yet this righteous king was made to suffer a horrible death, and misfortune on misfortune was heaped upon Judah. The proverb arose: "Our fathers have eaten sour grapes, and the children's teeth are set on edge." This conception appears in a still more drastic form in a remarkable passage of the Book of Jeremiah, where the answer is hurled at the head of the prophet, who is warning and exhorting his people: "When our fathers worshipped Baal and the stars, things went well with us, but since Josiah served the Lord only, things have gone ill." In opposition to such views, Ezekiel had now to bring forward proof that the judgment was deserved and unavoidable.

To this end, he passes in review the entire past of the people, and comes to the conclusion that it had been one long chain of direst ingratitude and shocking sin. Jerusalem is much worse than Samaria, has acted more sinfully than the Gentiles; even Sodom is justified by the iniquity of Jerusalem. Jerusalem is as a rusty pot, whose filthiness cannot be removed by being burnt out, but which must be thrown into the furnace, so that its metal may be purged and rendered fit for a new cast.

This appears heartless and is at times stated by Ezekiel with offensive severity. But to break up the new land required by Hosea and Jeremiah, the thorns and weeds must first be pitilessly dug out, and the earth upturned to its very depths by the ploughshares. Nothing else is Ezekiel's intention. By this painful process the ground is simply to be loosened for the new seed, for God takes no pleasure in the death of a sinner, but wishes rather that he be converted and live. And this conversion is quite possible; for the relation of God to man adjusts itself according to the relation of man to God. Now, here is the point where Ezekiel's creative genius is displayed. If religious personality be the true subject of religion, the inestimable value of every individual human soul follows directly from this fact. Here it is that the lever must be applied, and in Ezekiel thus prophecy is transformed into the pastoral care of souls.

The idea of pastoral care, and the recognition of it as a duty, is first found in Ezekiel. Even the Messiah does not appear to him in the pomp of a royal ruler, but as the good shepherd, who seeks him that is lost, goes after him that has strayed, binds up the wounded, and visits the sick and afflicted. Ezekiel considers this pastoral and educating office to be his vocation as prophet, and has conceived it with the sacred earnestness peculiar to himself: he feels himself to be personally responsible for the soul of every one of his fellow-countrymen: "If the wicked man sin, and thou givest him not warning, to save his life, the same wicked man shall die in his iniquity; but his blood will I require at thy hand. Yet if thou warn the wicked, and he turn not from his wickedness, nor from his wicked way, he shall die in his iniquity; but thou hast delivered thy soul." With these words God makes Ezekiel a prophet, or, as he has vividly expressed it, a "watchman over the house of Israel."

Such was the practical conclusion which Ezekiel drew from Jeremiah's religious conceptions, and by which he introduced into the religio-historical development of the world an entirely new force of imperishable importance and of incalculable consequences.

I spoke above, however, of a complement, of a corrective of the work of Jeremiah by Ezekiel, and this brings us to the point where Ezekiel exercised a powerful influence on the period which followed. Jeremiah with his religious subjectivism and individualism had spoken the final and conclusive word on the relation of the individual to God. But beyond individualism Jeremiah did not go. The conception of fellowship was altogether wanting in his views. He did not notice that great things on earth are only produced by union. Ezekiel, on the other hand, regarded it as the aim and task of his prophetic and pastoral mission to educate individuals not only to be religious, but also to be members of a community, which as such could not be subjectively determined only, but needed besides, definite objective rules and principles. The problem was, to preserve Israel in Babylon, to prevent the nation from being absorbed by the Gentiles. To this end Ezekiel insists that his people shall absolutely eschew the worship of the idols of their conquerors. He also discovers a means of directly worshipping God. Temple and sacrifices were wanting in the strange land, but they had the Sabbath, which appertained to no particular place nor land, which they could observe in Babylon just as well and in the same way as in Palestine. And so Ezekiel made the Sabbath the fundamental institution of Judaism, or, as he himself expresses it, "a sign between God and Israel, by which they shall know that it is God who sanctifies them." On every seventh day Israel shall feel itself to be the holy people of God.

Also in its mode of life Israel must prove itself a pure and holy people. Ezekiel warns his people against the sins of unchastity with greater emphasis than any of his predecessors. If the sanctification of wedded life and the purity of the family has ranked at all times as the costliest ornament and noblest treasure of the Jewish race, it is a possession, in which we cannot fail to recognise, more than any other, the seal which Ezekiel lastingly imprinted upon it. And moreover, Ezekiel urges and inculcates afresh the necessity of love towards brethren and neighbors. Every Israelite shall recognise in every other a brother and treat him with brotherly love, that the little band of dispersed and scattered exiles may be held together in ideal unity by this spiritual bond. If Ezekiel could only succeed in making of every individual a sanctified personality, who at the same time felt himself to be a member of a community and was steeped with the conviction that he could find true salvation only in this community, then would there be some hope of obtaining citizens worthy of the Kingdom of God, which was sure to come.

Ezekiel has given us a description of this future Kingdom of God, which ranks among the most remarkable creations of his book. It is the famous vision of the new Jerusalem, which forms the conclusion of the Book of Ezekiel. Here he essentially follows Deuteronomy. The service and worship of God are marked out most exactly, and the temple becomes, not only spiritually, but also materially, the centre of the whole nation and its life. The priests and Levites receive a definite portion of land as the material foundation of their existence.

Most noteworthy of all, however, is the future picture of the State in the vision of Ezekiel. In earlier speeches Ezekiel had expressed the hope that the future king would come of the house of David, though the king he pictures exhibits quite peculiar ecclesiastical characteristics. Now, however, there is no further mention of a king; he is merely called the prince. And what is his position? In the new Jerusalem crime is unknown, as God bestows on all a new heart and a new mind, and turns them into a people who walk in the way of his commandments, observe his laws, and act accordingly. The administration of justice, then, is no longer needed, and so one of the most important moral functions of the government dispensed with. Should, however, a crime or transgression actually occur, it must be atoned for by an ecclesiastical penance. Nor has the State need to provide for the external welfare of the people, for God gives all things bounteously now and no one is in want. Neither are measures for the external security of the country required, for this is a kingdom of everlasting peace, where war is no longer possible. Should a heathen nation dare to disturb this peace and stretch forth its hand against the Kingdom of God, God himself will interfere and in the fire of His wrath destroy the offender, so that Israel will only need to bury the corpses, and to burn with fire the weapons of the enemy, as described by Ezekiel in his wondrous vision of Gog, chief of the land of Magog.

In such conditions no function is left for the prince but that of representative of his people, and patron of the church. He has to look after the temple, and supply the materials of worship, for which purpose he can only collect from the people gifts of such things as are needful for the sacrifice : sheep, goats, bullocks, oxen, corn, wine, oil. All taxes are exclusively church taxes. The prince receives, so as not to oppress his people, nor exact unlawful tribute from them, a rich demesne of land, which he tills like every other Israelite. Also each individual tribe receives its determinate portion of the sacred land.

We have here for the first time in perfect distinctness the conception of a Kingdom of God, or, as we might also say, of an ecclesiastical State. The State is completely absorbed in the Church. Such is Ezekiel's new Jerusalem, and its name is "Here is God."

These ideas were feasible as long as the Babylonians, the Persians, and the Greeks deprived the Jews of all secular and governmental functions and discharged them themselves. Theocracy as a fact, for such we are wont to call this conception after a word coined by Josephus,—theocracy as a fact, realised in this world, needed as its complement and as its presupposition the conquest and government of the Jews by a foreign power. So soon, however, as Judah was enabled and obliged to form a national and political State, this contradiction asserted itself, and the tragical conflict arose which five hundred years later brought about the destruction of the State of the Maccabees.[1]

[1] Professor Cornill has devoted much time and labor to the prophet Ezekiel, the results of which were published in his works, *Der Prophet Ezechiel geschildert*, Heidelberg, 1882; *Das Buch des Propheten Ezechiel herausgegeben*, Leipsic, 1886. We regret to add that these books have not as yet been translated.—*Publisher.*

THE LITERARY ACHIEVEMENTS OF THE EXILE.

IN THE generation succeeding Ezekiel no prophet appeared in Babylon. Literary work followed other paths and other aims. The task which now devolved on the nation was the inventorying of the spiritual property of Israel; possibly the people also began at this time the collecting of the prophetic writings; at any rate they busied themselves extensively with the historical literature of the past.

The great philosopher Spinoza had observed that the historical books of the Old Testament, as now known to us, form a connected historical whole, narrating the history of the people of Israel from the creation of the world to the destruction of Jerusalem, and marshalling all materials under causal points of view of a distinctively religious character. This biassed but magnificent account of the past life of the chosen people was undertaken during the Babylonian exile, as we can discover from indubitable literary evidence.

At the time in question all the outward and specifically psychological conditions existed which favored such a bent of the mind. The destruction of State and nationality awakened a new interest in the past. As in the time of Germany's profoundest national disgrace, under the compulsory dominion of Napoleon, the love of the nation's all but forgotten past was rearoused to life, and people buried themselves with loving discernment in the rich depths of German minstrelsy, beginning once more to understand the German art of bygone days; as the Germans recalled to mind the names of Henry the Fowler, Frederick Barbarossa, Walther von der Vogelweide, and Albrecht Dürer: so, during the captivity in Babylon, the Jews lost themselves in the stories of Moses and David, Samuel and Elijah. They sought to lift themselves, by a study of their ancient greatness and by memories of the past, to a plane where they could withstand the present, and strengthen themselves for the future.

In thus contemplating the past, however, it was necessary to explain above all how the dread present had come to pass. For those exiled compilers and expounders of the ancient historical traditions of Israel, as for Ezekiel, the problem of all problems was the vindication of God, that is, a *theodicy*. And this theodicy, as in the case of Ezekiel, was conducted to show that all must have happened exactly as it did. All the evil which befell Israel is a punishment for sins and especially for the worship of idols. The sins of Jeroboam, who exhibited two golden calves at Dan and Bethel, hastened the destruction of Israel, and the sins of Manasseh, who had offered sacrifices in the temple of Jerusalem to Baal and to the stars, could only be atoned for by the destruction of Judah, despite the radical conversion and reforms of his grandson Josiah. Thus arose this prophetic exposition of the history of Israel, which converts the historian into a prophet with his eyes turned to the past.

But this historical writing has not only a theoretical side, looking back to the past, but also an eminently practical side, looking forward to the future. The Jews have a firm hope in the restoration of the nation, for which they possessed an infallible guarantee in the prophetical promise. Ever since Hosea the prophets had distinctly announced the judgment, but only seen in the judgment the necessary transition to the final salvation. On this latter they counted, and prepared themselves for its arrival. And this prophetic history of the past shall be both a warning and a guidance for the future. The new Israel risen again from the tomb of captivity shall avoid the sins and errors of the old Israel, which caused her destruction. We have thus in the historical work of the exile a sort of applied prophecy, whose influence and efficacy were perhaps even greater than that of prophecy itself.

We see thus that the exiles lived in constant hope. Nor had they long to wait for its fulfilment. Seventy years was the time fixed by Jeremiah as the period of the Chaldean rule. But forty-eight years after the destruction of Jerusalem the kingdom of Babylon had ceased to exist, and, in the year following, the new king granted to the exiles the long-wished-for permission to return to the land of their fathers. The Babylonian kingdom rested wholly on the person of its founder, and only survived his death twenty-three years.

Nebuchadnezzar is styled by modern historians, not unjustly, "the great." He is the most towering personality in the whole history of the ancient Orient, and a new era begins with him. The greatness of the man consists in the manner in which he conceived his vocation as monarch. Nebuchadnezzar was a warrior as great as any that had previously existed. He had gained victories and made conquests equal to those of the mightiest rulers before him. But he never mentions a word of his brilliant achievements in any of the numerous inscriptions we have of him. We know of his deeds only through the accounts given by those whom he conquered, and from strangers who admired him. He himself tells us only of buildings and works of peace, which he completed with the help of the gods, whom he worshipped with genuine reverence. The gods bestowed on him sovereignty, that he might become the benefactor of his people and subjects. He rebuilt destroyed cities, restored ruined temples, laid out canals and ponds, regulated the course of rivers, and established harbors, so as to open safe ways and new roads for commerce and traffic. We see in this a clear conception of the moral duties of the State, where its primary object is to become a power for civilisation.

Forty-three years were allotted to Nebuchadnezzar, in which he reigned to the welfare of humanity. He died in the year 561. Destiny denied to him a befitting successor. His son, Evil Merodach, was murdered two years after, for his atrocities and dissoluteness, by his brother-in-law, Nergalsharezer, who must have been a descendant of the older line of Babylonian kings. At his death four years later, Nergalsharezer was able to bequeath the empire intact to his son Labasi-marduk. But as this king, according to the Babylonian historian Berosus, exhibited a thoroughly bad character, he was slain by his courtiers after nine months of sovereignty, and Nabu-nahid ascended the throne, 555 B. C., as the last of the Babylonian kings. Nabu-nahid, or Nabonidus, appears to have been a personally mild and just ruler, with literary and antiquarian tastes, to which we owe much that is important. But a storm lowered over his head, which was soon to destroy with the rapidity of lightning both himself and his kingdom.

Cyrus, the Median viceroy of that primitive and robust nation of hunters and horsemen, the Persians, had shaken off the Median yoke. In the year 550 he had conquered and taken prisoner Astyages, the last Median king, and captured his capital Ecbatana. Four years later, Lydia, the powerful neighboring empire of Cyrus, succumbed to his resistless courage and energy.

And now the destruction, or at least the conquest, of the Babylonian empire was but a question of time. A mighty seething was taking place among the Jewish exiles. Anxiously and full of confidence they awaited the saviour and avenger who would destroy Babylon and again restore Jerusalem. And in this period of the gathering storm, the stillness before the tempest, prophecy again lifted up its voice in one of its noblest and grandest representatives, the great Unknown, who wrote the concluding portions of the Book of Isaiah, and who is therefore called the Second, or Deutero-Isaiah.

DEUTERO-ISAIAH.

IT IS now generally admitted, and may be regarded as one of the best established results of Old Testament research, that the portion of our present Book of Isaiah, which embraces Chapters 40 to 66, did not emanate from the prophet Isaiah known to us, but is the work of an unknown prophet of the period towards the end of the Babylonian captivity.

In many respects this Second or Deutero-Isaiah must be accounted the most brilliant jewel of prophetic literature. In him are gathered together as in a focus all the great and noble meditations of the prophecy which preceded him, and he reflects them with the most gorgeous refraction, and with the most beauteous play of light and color. In style he is a genius of the first rank, a master of language, and a proficient in diction equalled by few. One feels almost tempted to call him the greatest among the prophets, were it not that we find in him the most distinct traces that the Israelitish prophecy had reached once for all its culminating point in Jeremiah, and that we are now starting on the downward slope. These traces, it is true, are scattered and sporadic in Deutero-Isaiah, but they are the more striking in connexion with a mind of such pre-eminence. Prophecy has now a drop of foreign blood in its veins, which the first Isaiah or Jeremiah would have repudiated with indignation. The influence and views of Deuteronomy, which first disintegrated and then completely stifled prophecy, now begin to make themselves felt.

The fundamental theme and the burden of his message is told by Deutero-Isaiah in the first words of his book, which also form the beginning of Händel's *Messiah*, and are well-known to every lover of music in the wondrously solemn strains of the master:

"Comfort ye, comfort ye my people, saith your God. Speak ye comfortably to Jerusalem and cry unto her that her day of trial is accomplished and that her iniquity is pardoned; for she hath received of the Lord's hand double for all her sins."

In the wilderness the way shall be prepared for God and his people returning to their home:

"Prepare ye in the wilderness the way of the Lord, make straight in the desert a highway for our God. Every valley shall be exalted, and every mountain and hill shall be made low; and the crooked shall be made straight and the rough places plain. For now the glory of the Lord shall be revealed, and all flesh shall see it, for the mouth of the Lord hath spoken it."

And all these wonders shall be fulfilled, for no

power in man can hinder God's work, because his promise remains eternally.

"All flesh is grass, and all the splendor thereof is as the flower of the field. The grass withereth, the flower fadeth: because the spirit of the Lord bloweth upon it. The grass withereth, the flower fadeth, but the word of our God shall stand forever."

And now Jerusalem lying in its ruins is addressed, and the joyful message shouted to the other Jewish towns that were demolished:

"O Zion that bringeth good tidings, get thee up into a high mountain. O Jerusalem that bringeth good tidings, lift up thy voice with strength; lift it up, be not afraid; say unto the cities of Judah, Behold your God! Behold the Lord God will come with strong hand and his arm shall rule free in his omnipotence: behold his reward is with him, and his recompense before him. He shall feed his flock like a shepherd; he shall gather the lambs in his arms, and carry them in his bosom, and shall gently lead those that are with young."

What fills the prophet with this hope, that which has given him the assurance that now the salvation promised by God is about to be accomplished, are the victories and deeds of Cyrus, by which the king had proved himself to be the chosen weapon, the executor of the divine judgment on Babylon.

"Who hath raised up the man from the east, in whose footsteps victory follows, hath given the nations before him, and made him rule over kings? hath given them as dust to his sword, and as the driven stubble to his bow? He pursueth them, and passeth on safely, even by ways that his feet have never trodden."

"I have raised up him from the north and he shall come: from the rising of the sun shall he call upon my name, and he shall come upon princes as upon mortar, and as the potter treadeth clay."

"I have raised him up for victory and I will make straight all his ways; he shall build my city again, and he shall let my exiles go free."

"I shall call a ravenous bird from the east, and the man that executeth my counsel from a far country; yea, I have spoken it, I will also bring it to pass; I have purposed it, I will also do it."

God loves him, and has chosen him to perform his pleasure on Babylon and execute his judgment on the Chaldeans.

"I, even I, have spoken; yea, I have called him, I have brought him hither, and his way shall be prosperous."

Cyrus is even called directly by name, so that there may not be the slightest doubt as to the upshot of the matter:

"I am the Lord that saith of Cyrus: He is my shepherd and shall perform all my pleasure, even saying to Jerusalem, Thou shalt be built, and to the temple, thy foundation shall be laid again."

"Thus saith the Lord to his anointed, to Cyrus,

whose right hand I have strengthened, to subdue nations before him; and the doors shall open before him, and the gates shall not be shut. I myself will go before thee and make the rugged places plain; I will break in pieces the gates of brass, and cut in sunder the bars of iron; and I will give thee the treasures of darkness, and hidden riches of secret places, that thou mayest know that I, the Lord, which call thee by name, am the God of Israel."

Here the prophet calls the Persian conqueror by the most honorable names, "Shepherd," even "anointed of God," and here must be considered the curious fact, that he nowhere speaks of a future Messiah of the house of David, but that he is always concerned simply with God on the one hand, and with Israel and Jerusalem on the other. This seems to have met with lively opposition from his first hearers. They cannot bring themselves to find in a Gentile the executor of that, which according to general expectation the ideal Son of David should accomplish; and thus Deutero-Isaiah in a very remarkable passage chides their questionings and anxieties, which is tantamount to a criticism of the plan of God, who has decided upon this Persian king as his shepherd and as his anointed. And that leads us to a cardinal feature in Deutero-Isaiah,—namely, the stress he lays on the omnipotence of God, and which the prophet never wearies of repeating in ever newer and loftier variations:

"Who hath measured the waters in the hollow of

his hand, and meted out heaven with the span, and comprehended the dust of the earth in a measure and weighed the mountains in scales, and the hills in a balance?"

"Behold the nations before him are as a drop of a bucket and are counted as the small dust of a balance: behold he weigheth the isles as dust. And Lebanon is not sufficient for wood to burn, nor the beasts thereof sufficient for a burnt offering. All nations before him are as nothing: and they are counted to him less than nothing, and vanity."

"It is he that sitteth upon the circle of the earth, and the inhabitants thereof are as grasshoppers; that stretcheth out the heavens as a curtain, and spreadeth them out like a tent to dwell in."

"Lift up your eyes to heaven. Who hath created this? He that bringeth out their host by number and calleth them all by names; for that he is strong in power, not one faileth."

This omnipotent God of Israel is the only God in Heaven and on earth, everlasting, eternal, the first and the last, and beside Him there is no God. Deutero-Isaiah lays special emphasis on this point. No one has held up to scorn more bitterly than he the idols of the heathen, and proved their emptiness and impotence.

"The workman melteth a graven image, and the goldsmith spreadeth it over with gold, and casteth thereon silver chains. He that is too impoverished for such an outlay chooseth a tree that will not rot; and seeketh unto him a cunning workman to prepare a graven image, that shall not rock."

"They helped every one his neighbour and every one said to his brother, Be of good courage. So the workman encouraged the goldsmith, and he that smootheth with the hammer him that smiteth the anvil, saying of the soldering, It is good: and he fasteneth it with nails, that it should not be moved."

"They lavish gold out of the bag, and weigh silver in the balance, and hire a goldsmith, and he maketh it a god: they fall down, yea, they worship it. They bear him upon the shoulder, they carry him, and set him in his place and he standeth; from his place shall he not remove: yea, one shall cry unto him, yet he cannot answer, nor save him out of his trouble."

And, again, in the principal passage:

"Who hath formed a god, or molten a graven image that is profitable for nothing? Behold all his fellows shall be ashamed, for the workmen they are men. The smith with the tongs both worketh in the coals and fashioneth with hammers, and worketh it with the strength of his arms; he groweth hungry and his strength faileth: he drinketh no water and is faint. The carpenter stretcheth out his rule, he marketh it out with a line, he fitteth it with planes, and he marketh it out with the compass, and shapeth it after the figure of a man, according to the beauty of a man, to dwell in a house. He heweth him down cedars and taketh the holm-tree and the oak which he strengtheneth for himself among the trees of the forest; he planteth a fir-tree and the rain doth nourish it, that it shall be for a man to burn. And he taketh thereof and warmeth himself; yea, he kindleth it and maketh bread; yea, he maketh a god and worshippeth it; he maketh it a graven image and falleth down thereto. He burneth part thereof in the fire; with part thereof he eateth flesh; he roasteth roast and is satisfied; yea, he warmeth himself and saith, Aha, I am warm, I have felt the fire: And the residue thereof he maketh a god, even his graven image: he falleth down unto it and worshippeth it, and prayeth unto it, and saith, Deliver me; for thou art my god. . . . And none considereth in his heart, neither is there knowledge nor understanding to say, I have burned part of it in the fire; yea, also I have baked bread upon the coals thereof; I have roasted flesh and eaten it: and shall I make the residue thereof an abomination? shall I fall down to the stock of a tree?"

And the exclusive divinity of this God of Israel is now proved by Deutero-Isaiah most characteristically from the prophecy: he is the only One who has previously foretold the future:

"Thus saith the Lord, the King of Israel, and his redeemer, the Lord of hosts. I am the first and I am the last; and beside me there is no God. Who is as I? Let him stand forth and say it and declare it, and set it opposite to me. And the things that are coming, and that shall come to pass, let them declare. Fear ye not, neither be afraid: have I not declared unto thee of old, and shewed it? ye even are my witnesses, whether there be a God, whether there be a rock beside me?"

This God of prophecy, whose predictions never fail, had long foretold that Babylon must fall, and He, the Almighty, before whom the people are as nothing, He will now carry out His plan, through Cyrus, His shepherd and His anointed. The impending destruction of the Babylonian tyrant, of his kingdom, and of his city, is described in the most vivid colors of hatred and scorn. And then shall take place the return of Israel to the land of its fathers. God himself heads the procession and makes in the wilderness a safe way through shady trees and rippling fountains, that they may build at last the new Jerusalem, whose splendor the prophet depicts in the most gorgeous colors.

"For the mountains shall depart and the hills be removed, but my kindness shall not depart from thee, neither shall the covenant of my peace be removed, saith the Lord that hath mercy on thee. O thou afflicted, tossed with tempests, and not comforted, behold I will set thy stones in fair colors and lay thy foundations with sapphires. And I will make thy pinnacles of rubies, and thy gates of carbuncles, and all thy border of precious stones. And all who build thee shall be taught of the Lord and great shall be the peace of thy children. In righteousness shalt thou be established; thou shalt be far from oppression for thou shalt not fear, and from terror for it shall not come near thee. If bands gather together against thee, it shall not be from me: and whosoever shall gather together against thee shall fall because of thee." "I will make thy officers peace, and thine exactors righteousness . . . and thou shalt call thy walls Salvation, and thy gates Praise. The sun shall be no more thy light by day; neither for brightness shall the moon give light unto thee; but the Lord shall be unto thee an everlasting light, and thy God thy glory. . . . Thy people also shall be all righteous; they shall inherit the land forever, the branch of my planting, the work of my hands, that I may be glorified."

Brilliant as all this is, however, it is in a manner only a secondary achievement of Deutero-Isaiah. His special and fundamental conception is different, and infinitely more profound than this. He adopted the idea, first clearly conceived by the original Isaiah, of a world's history, but widened it and deepened it by combination with one of Jeremiah's thoughts. According to Jeremiah, all men and all nations are destined and called upon to turn to God and become His children. Deutero-Isaiah sees in this the final aim of the history of the world, towards which its entire development and guidance strives. "My house shall be called a house of prayer unto all nations."

Now, this gives to him an entirely new foundation

for his contemplation of Israel. Israel alone knows and possesses the true God. Only through Israel can the other nations learn to know Him, and thus Israel becomes the servant and messenger of God, the laborer and herald of God to man. Israel is to mankind what the prophet is to Israel. God is the God of the whole earth, and Israel His prophet for the whole earth. Thus may we sum up most succinctly the theology of Deutero-Isaiah. He says:

"But thou, Israel, my servant, Jacob whom I have chosen, the seed of Abraham, my friend; thou whom I have taken hold of from the ends of the earth, and called thee from the corners thereof, and said unto thee, Thou art my servant; I have chosen thee and not cast thee away; fear then not for I am with thee; be not dismayed, for I am thy God: I will strengthen thee; yea, I will help thee; yea, I will uphold thee with the right hand of my righteousness. Behold all they that are incensed against thee shall be ashamed and confounded: they that strive with thee shall be as nothing, and shall perish. . . . For I the Lord thy God will hold thy right hand, saying unto thee, Fear not; I will help thee. Fear not, thou worm Jacob, thou maggot Israel; I will help thee, saith the Lord, and thy redeemer, the Holy One of Israel."

"It is too light a thing that I should raise up the tribes of Jacob, and restore the preserved of Israel: I will also give thee for a light to the Gentiles, that thou mayest be my salvation unto the ends of the earth."

"Behold my servant, whom I uphold; mine elect, in whom my soul delighteth; I have put my spirit upon him; he shall bring forth judgment to the Gentiles. . . . A bruised reed shall he not break, and the smoking flax shall he not quench: he shall bring forth judgment in truth. He shall not quench, nor shall he bruise, till he have set judgment in the earth, and the isles shall wait for his law."

And here Deutero-Isaiah obtains a clue to the enigmatical history of Israel. All Israel's sufferings have been borne in its vocation as servant of God. "Who is blind, but my servant? or deaf, as my messenger that I send? who is blind as my trusted one, and deaf as the Lord's servant?"

But this also did God will and suffer. In the unworthiness of the instrument does the splendor, the greatness of God disclose itself, who knows how to fulfil His plans in mysterious ways. Even in Israel those only become the servant of God who have returned to Jacob, who are of broken heart and contrite spirit; and thus the tribulations of Israel serve the great universal plan, in that they educate Israel for its mission in the world, its everlasting, high vocation. Israel is the suffering servant of God, on whom the punishment falls, that the salvation of the world may come to pass, and through whose wounds all shall be saved. Israel's forced sufferings were borne for its own and for the world's salvation, that Israel, purified and refined through sorrows, might become a light to the Gentiles and a blessing to the whole world.

A more magnificent theology of history, if I may be allowed the expression, than that of Deutero-Isaiah, has never been given.

And yet this sublime mind cannot withdraw itself altogether from the influences of the time, and so Deutero-Isaiah falls short of the eminence of Jeremiah, and begins the declining line of prophecy. Jeremiah's circumcision of the heart becomes in him the circumcision of the flesh; to him the sanctity of the new Jerusalem mainly consists in that it shall not be inhabited by the uncircumcised and the impure; the converted Gentiles he looks upon only as Jews of the second order. In that Israel had to suffer for the world, shall it in the concluding age of salvation rule over the world. Kings shall lie prostrate before this people and lick the dust from off their feet. All the nations shall bring their treasures and riches to Jerusalem. The people or kingdom which does not do homage to Israel shall perish; yea, all nations shall worship Israel, and do menial service for Israel, tend its flocks, and till its fields and vineyards, whilst Israel shall consume the riches of the nations, and be made a praise in the earth. Jeremiah could not have written such sentences. Here we remark that with Deutero-Isaiah we are no longer in Israel, but have reached Judaism.

The deliverance of Israel so fervidly hoped for and foretold with such assurance by Deutero-Isaiah did in reality take place. With the lightning-like rapidity peculiar to him, Cyrus had also overthrown the kingdom of Babylon. On the 3d of November, 538, he made his triumphal entry into Babylon. The kingdom of Nebuchadnezzar ceased to exist. And within a year after the capture of Babylon the new ruler actually gave the exiles permission to return to Jerusalem. In the spring of 537 B. C. they began their journey, and with it begins a new chapter in the history of Israel and of prophecy.

THE RETURN FROM THE CAPTIVITY.

CYRUS, the conqueror and new ruler of Babylon, at once gave the Jewish exiles permission to return to their native land, and supported and helped them in every way. We have no reason to doubt the assertion that he provided the means for rebuilding the demolished temple from the funds of the Persian treasury, and that he ordered the sacred vessels of the ancient temple which had been plundered by the Chaldeans, so far as they still existed or were recognisable, to be returned to the homeward-bound Israelites.

The question has been raised, why Cyrus should have exhibited such sympathy for the Jewish exiles and espoused so cordially their cause, and the reason of it has been sought in a certain supposed affinity between the Ahura-Mazda religion avowed by Cyrus and his Persians, and the God-belief of the Israelites. In point of fact a certain similarity may be traced between the pure and profound Persian worship of light and the belief of the Jewish exiles in Babylon, whilst, on the other hand, to a Mazda-Yasnian, like Cyrus, the Babylonian cult must have appeared in the highest degree unsympathetic and ludicrous.

But Cyrus was not a sentimental man, and religious fanaticism was as foreign to him as to his people. We have to recognise in the liberation of the Jews merely a political action, the reason of which is very apparent. Now that Babylon had been overthrown, there existed but one powerful state bordering on the kingdom of Persia, and that was the old land of the pyramids—Egypt, which just at this time was enjoying a new lease of vigor under the long and prosperous reign of Amasis, and was taking an important part in politics. As early as the year 547 Egypt had joined a powerful coalition against the young and rising kingdom of Persia; long before, the Assyrians had fought against Egypt and temporarily subdued it, and likewise Nebuchadnezzar had waged war against this country. It lay in the logic of facts and circumstances, accordingly, that sooner or later hostilities between the two neighboring powers must break out; and therefore it was the most natural thing in the world that such a clear-sighted and far-seeing man as Cyrus should prepare for it. The restoration of Jerusalem and of Judah, then, was a mere link in the chain of these preparations. Judæa was the province bordering on Egypt, and Jerusalem the natural basis of operations for a campaign directed against the valley of the Nile. We can, therefore, well understand that it appeared desirable to Cyrus to know that a people dwelt there who was bound to him by the most powerful ties of gratitude, and on whose faithfulness and devotion he could confidently rely.

If Cyrus laid stress on the religious element and proved himself a worshipper of the God of the Jews, his attitude in this respect simply coincides with his maxims of government, as we may show by documentary evidence. A considerable number of inscriptions concerning Cyrus exist, which he as king of Babylon ordered to be made in the old Babylonian cuneiform character, and in these Cyrus appears as the most devout servant and sincere worshipper of the Babylonian gods. He returns thanks to Merodach and to Nebo for the protection accorded to him, and grants special privileges to their temples and priests. The conduct of Cyrus towards the Jewish exiles must be considered from this twofold point of view, which does not exclude the additional possibility that in their fervid expectation of the fall of the Babylonian tyrant, the Jews took an active part in the operations and both countenanced and aided Cyrus and his Persians in their enterprise against Babylon, for which the Persians showed themselves thankful.

In the spring of the year 537 B. C. the Israelites began their homeward march. They numbered about 50,000 souls and were evidently members of all the families of the house of Judah. They were under the leadership of the Persian commissary Sheshbazzar. The government and management of internal affairs was lodged in a council of twelve confidential advisors, among whom and occupying the highest offices were Zerubbabel, the grandson of King Jehoiachin, and Joshua, the grandson of Seraiah, the last priest of the temple of Jerusalem put to death under Nebuchadnezzar.

It has often been supposed that the worldly-minded of the Jewish nation remained behind in Babylon, in sure and comfortable positions, from unwillingness to risk the dangers of the march, or the hardships of laying out and newly settling a devastated country. But this view is totally false and in contradiction to well-established facts. We shall soon see that the Jews who remained behind, in the end really led the work of reform, and victoriously carried to completion the rehabilitation of the religious system against the will of those who returned in 537.

Immediately on the arrival of the exiles the altar was erected on the sacred spot where once had stood the sacrificial altar of the temple of Solomon, and the autumn festival of the year 537 could accordingly be celebrated with a solemn oblation to the God of Israel. Unfortunately we have only meagre and incomplete details regarding the 370 years which intervene between this event and the outbreak of the Maccabæan revolt; only isolated moments and events are at all well known to us, and these, although they throw a ray of light now and then into the dense obscurity of this period, yet ofttimes present more puzzles than they solve.

In 537 the cult was restored, but the most definite and indubitable evidence forces us to conclude that no attempt was made to rebuild the temple for seventeen years. On the other hand, highly momentous transformations must have taken place within the priesthood; for in the year 520 we suddenly find a high-priest of whom there is no premonitory trace in the Israel of the pre-exilic period, and of whom absolutely nothing is known either in Deuteronomy, or by Ezekiel.

I regret that I am unable to enter more minutely into this matter, for it is as important as it is interesting. It is to be observed that in the year 520 B. C. prophecy once more awoke. And here again a great historical crisis was its origin. Cambyses, the degenerate son and successor of the great Cyrus, had indeed subdued Egypt in 525, and thus inserted the keystone in the arch of the Persian empire; but he was very near destroying it by his cruelty and tyranny. In 522 the Magus Gaumata gave himself out to be the brother of Cambyses whom the latter had secretly put to death, and called upon the Persian people to rid themselves of this monster. Cambyses marched against him, but committed suicide in Hamath in Syria, leaving no son. The Magus ruled for nearly a year unmolested, till Darius, who was directly connected with the royal house through a branch line, claimed his rights as heir, and aided by the noblest families of Persia, put the Magus to death in the autumn of the year 521. That was the signal for uprisings throughout the whole empire. Excitement reigned everywhere. Two full years Darius had to struggle with difficulties of every kind, till at last he succeeded in restoring order and consolidating the kingdom of Persia, a consolidation which lasted more than two centuries.

In this restless and seething period prophecy was again aroused. Suddenly Zerubbabel of the house of David appears as the Persian viceroy in Judæa. It is possible that Darius did this to win over the sympathies of the Jews, and to assure himself of their help at a period when his sovereignty was gravely threatened.

In the year 520 a bad harvest seems to have brought famine and hunger into the land; and at this crisis appeared an aged and venerable man, Haggai, who had seen with his own eyes the old temple and the old Jerusalem, and who must therefore have been in his seventies, with words of warning and exhortation. The famine had been the punishment of God for that the people dwelt in ceiled houses, whilst His house lay waste. Undaunted and unconcerned should they go to work, for a grand future was in store for this new temple, and Zerubbabel himself should be their Messiah. Saith Haggai:

"Yet now be strong, O Zerubbabel, be strong, O

Joshua, be strong all ye people, and work, for I am with you, saith the Lord of hosts ... and my spirit remaineth among you ... For thus saith the Lord of hosts: Yet once, it is a little while, and I will shake the heavens, and the earth, and the sea, and the dry land. And I will shake all nations, and the valuable things of all nations shall come, and I will fill this house with glory. The silver is mine, and the gold is mine, and the latter glory of this house will be greater than the former, and in this place will I give peace."

And to Zerubbabel specially He saith:

"I will shake the heavens and the earth, and I will overthrow the throne of kingdoms, and I will destroy the strength of the kingdoms of the heathen; and I will overthrow the chariots and those that ride in them, and the horses and their riders shall come down, every one by the sword of his brother. In that day will I take thee, O Zerubbabel, my servant, and I will make thee as a signet: for I have chosen thee."

As we are told by Haggai, the cornerstone of the new temple was actually laid on the 24th of December, 520. We can plainly see the influence and reflexion of the ideas of Isaiah and Deutero-Isaiah in Haggai. Haggai has given us nothing of his own. Yet in its simple and unpretentious style his little book has something peculiarly touching in it, and brings before us vividly and immediately the feelings and views of his time.

Contemporaneously with Haggai appeared another prophet with the same views and with the same aims—Zechariah. His book has the same subject as that of Haggai: the rebuilding of the temple and the future Messianic kingdom of Zerubbabel. But in a literary point of view Zechariah is highly remarkable and unique. He has abandoned the old style of prophecy, which was that of the discourse or sermon, and depicts in its stead visions which he has seen, and which are explained to him by an angel. Zechariah clothes his ideas in mysteriously symbolical forms, which is indubitable proof that prophecy has loosed itself from its natural soil and developed into a purely literary creation. It may be compared to a book-drama of to-day. In all these productions of art the emotional and passionate elements are wanting which are to be found in the older prophetic writings, and which Haggai himself still knew how to preserve. Just as religion since Deuteronomy had become a book-religion, so now prophecy became purely literary in form. The thought of a personal and direct influence has totally disappeared.

The altered relation of the prophet towards God is also noteworthy. Whilst the older prophets feel themselves to be completely one with God, who is ever present and living in them, God now grows more and more transcendent; the direct personal intercourse of the prophet with God ceases; an angel steps in between, who communes with him as an intermediary.

Zechariah has at his disposal a rich and lively fantasy, and his book is highly interesting and in its kind excellent; but it is nevertheless a clear witness of the growing deterioration of prophecy.

Especially typical of the conceptions of the time is the first of his visions. A man stands among myrtle trees, to whom come four apocalyptical riders on four horses of different colors. These horsemen have been sent to walk to and fro through the earth and bring news of what takes place. And they answer and say: "We have walked to and fro through the earth, and behold, all the earth sitteth still and is at rest." Then the angel who explains the vision to the prophet exclaims: "O Lord of hosts, how long wilt thou not have mercy on Jerusalem and on the cities of Judah, against which thou hast had indignation these threescore and ten years?"

From the revolution, from the overthrow of all existing circumstances, Israel expects the realisation of its hopes of the future, the destruction of the kingdoms of this world and the foundation of the Kingdom of God. The events of the world were followed with anxious curiosity; whenever a storm gathered on the political horizon, men believed they saw in it the signs of the great future. Thus was this unrestful and critical period of the Persian empire a time of great exitement among the Jews, and was looked upon by them all in the same way. We learn from Zechariah the remarkable fact that the Jews who had remained behind in Babylon sent at this time a golden crown to Jerusalem to be worn by Zerubbabel as the future Messiah King. It is the electrification, so to speak, of an atmosphere heavy with storm, which we feel in the Book of Zechariah.

But all hopes were in vain. Darius proved himself equal to the situation; the Persian empire stood firmer than ever, and all remained as before. In the meanwhile the building of the temple made rapid progress; the Satrap of the province, on the other side of the Euphrates, to which Judah belonged, named Tatnai, asked officially for orders. Darius expressly permitted the completion and also promised state-aid. The Satrap Tatnai took the matter up, and on the third day of March, 515, the new temple was completed after four and a half years' work.

EZRA AND NEHEMIAH.

LET us consider, now, the feelings with which the Jewish people regarded this new temple of their God. Elated they were not, they could not be. On the contrary they must have felt deeply depressed, for in a certain measure they had been disappointed in all their hopes. The worst of all was not that this new temple in no way rivalled the magnificence and splendor of the old temple of Solomon. A still heavier sorrow weighed down their hearts. God had broken his word, had not fulfilled his promises, had abandoned his people. What had not the prophets foretold, as destined to happen after the Babylonian captivity? What brilliant images had they not drawn of the future Israel and the new Jerusalem? Deutero-Isaiah especially had forced these hopes to the topmost pitch, and a reaction could not fail to take place, —a reaction of the saddest and most painful kind. When the reality was compared with the gorgeous predictions of the prophets, the effect must have been overpowering.

What change had taken place? None. The Persians had taken the place of the Babylonians, but the Gentile power remained as formidable as ever. Returned to the old land of their fathers, they had to struggle hard for existence; the conditions of life were extremely meagre; only a very small part of Jerusalem had been rebuilt, a wretched, unfortified country-town with an indigent population, not even the shadow of what it once had been, which in the fantasy of this posthumous generation assumed ever more brilliant colors. And this God who had not kept his promise, who had in no way shown his power, demanded yet more at their hands. He called for a costly cultus and ritual, and a mode of life governed by the harshest laws. Was it not then better to become even as the Gentiles, whose power flourished unabated and who enjoyed unbounded happiness? Thus must disappointment and bitterness have filled the hearts of the Jews, and showed itself in indifference or even in enmity towards this deceitful, powerless Deity. And that these moods gradually did gain possession of the majority of the people in Jerusalem and Judæa, and that particularly the leading men and priests were dominated by them, we have classic proof in a book of prophecy written fifty years after Zechariah, and known to us as Malachi. Malachi describes to us most faithfully the temper of the Jews who had strayed from God, and who sought through careless indifference or frivolous mockery to disregard the misery of their time.

"Ye have wearied the Lord with your words. Yet ye say, Wherein have we wearied him? In that ye say, Every one that doeth evil is good in the sight of the Lord and he delighteth in them; else, where is the God of judgment? . . . Your words have been stout against me, saith the Lord. Yet ye say, Wherein have we spoken against thee? Ye have said, It is vain to serve God: and what profit is it that we have kept his charge, and that we have walked mournfully before the Lord Zebaoth? And now must we call the proud happy; yea, they that work wickedness are built up; yea, they tempt God and are delivered."

And how in such moods religious duties were performed, Malachi relates most drastically:

"A son honoureth his father, and a servant his master: but if I be a father where is my honour? and if I be a master, where is my fear? saith the Lord Zebaoth unto you, O priests, that despise my name. And ye say, Wherein have we despised thy name? Ye offer polluted bread upon mine altar . . . thinking, The table of the Lord is contemptible. And when ye offer the blind for sacrifice it is no evil, and when ye offer the lame and sick, it is no evil. Present it now unto thy governor; will he be pleased with thee? or show thee favour? . . . Ye have brought the blind, the lame, and the sick: thus ye bring the offering: should I accept this of your hand? saith the Lord. Cursed be the deceiver which hath in his flock a male beast that he has vowed, but sacrificeth unto the Lord a blemished thing; for I am a great King, saith the Lord Zebaoth, and my name is honoured among the nations."

On the other hand, Malachi lays great stress upon the judgment, which is sure to come, and which will show that devotion and fear of God are not empty dreams. But first, God must cause a purifying and refining of his people to take place, and will send Elijah, the prophet, for this purpose, prior to the coming of the great and dreadful day.

We cast here a glance into an exceedingly momentous crisis. Should such moods gain full sway, should they succeed in laying hold of the whole people, then there was an end of Judah and of religion. But Malachi speaks of men who fear the Lord, who are inscribed in God's remembrance-book, of a party, who in opposition to those moods and strivings clung all the more closely to the despised and rejected religion. These did not deny the events and causes on which this indifference and scepticism were based, but drew from them quite different conclusions.

"The proud and they that work wickedness," as Malachi terms them, sought to lay the blame of the non-fulfilment of the hoped for prophecies on God, who either could not or would not perform them; the devout lay the blame on themselves. They did not ask what it was incumbent on *God* to do, but what *they* should and could have done. It was foolishness and sin to doubt God's omnipotence. If he had not performed his promise, he had been unable to do so because of Israel itself: the nation was not yet fully worthy of its great future. Therefore, they must strive to repair their shortcoming by redoubled piety. This is the legalism and the "salvation by works" of the later Judaism.

We shall never rightly understand, nor rightly value this tendency, until we thoroughly comprehend its origin. That origin was the Messianic hope. Israel lives entirely in the future, entirely in hope, and is determined to leave nothing undone to hasten that future; it will, so to speak, wrest it from God, compel him to perform his promises, by sweeping away the only impediment to their fulfilment.

But this little band of devout men in Jerusalem could not have brought about of themselves the triumph of their intentions; help was necessary from outside. That help was granted, and from Babylon. The Jews who had remained in Babylon had outstripped those who had returned to Jerusalem. An entire school of men had been established there, who worked out the ideas of Ezekiel, and drew the last conclusions of Deuteronomy. The work of this school had found its literary embodiment in the juridical parts of the first books of the Pentateuch, usually known as the fundamental writing, or priestly code, to which, for example, the whole of the third book of Moses, Leviticus, belongs. This is the legislation, which is usually regarded as the specific work of Moses, and which naturally presents itself to our mind when we speak of Mosaism.

This book was written in Babylon about 500 B.C., and was regarded there as important and sacred. The hour was soon to come in which it should accomplish its mighty mission. The Jews of Babylon were thoroughly acquainted with the events that happened in Judæa; and thus the extremely serious turn that matters were taking there could not remain concealed from them. They determined on taking an active part. Ezra, a near relative of the high-priest's family of Jerusalem, and sprung from the same tribe, placed himself at the head of the undertaking. He obtained from the Persian king, Artaxerxes (Longhand), a decree giving him full power to reform matters in Judah and Jerusalem, "according to the book of the law of God, which was in his hand" (that is, the so-called priestly code).

On the 12th of April, 458, the Jews left Babylon and arrived in Jerusalem on the first day of August. They numbered about 1700 men; the figure of the women and children is not given. Ezra found matters in Jerusalem to be far worse and more comfortless than he had feared. Nevertheless, he began his work of reformation, but had to quit the field owing to the violent and bitter resistance which he met with, till thirteen years later a man after his own heart, Nehemiah, a Babylonian Jew who had attained the position of favorite and cup-bearer to King Artaxerxes, begged for the post of Persian governor of Judæa, which had become vacant. And now the strong arm of the law was placed at the disposal of the work of reform, and both Ezra and Nehemiah took up with vigor and zeal the neglected task. In October, 444, a great gathering of the people was held. Here the nation bound itself by oath to Ezra's book of the law, as it had done 177 years previously under Josiah to Deuteronomy. Still many a hard and bitter struggle was to be fought, but Ezra and Nehemiah carried their cause through, and broke down all opposition. Those who could not adapt themselves to the new condition of affairs, left the country to escape in foreign lands the compulsion of the law.

These events are of immeasurable importance and of uncommon interest. Through them Judaism was definitively established. Ezra and Nehemiah are its founders.

It is not to be denied, much less concealed, that this Judaism of Ezra and Nehemiah displays few engaging traits. If soon after its establishment we notice that the Jew is everywhere an object of hatred and distrust, the fact is owing to the distinctive stamp of his religion. When the Jew cut himself off brusquely and contemptuously from all non-Jews, when all men who did not belong to his religious community were for him but heathens, unclean persons with whom he could not eat, or even come in contact, without thereby becoming himself unclean, when he appeared before them with the pretension of alone being the good man, the beloved of God, whilst all others had only anger and destruction to expect at God's hand, and when he thirsted for this as the final object of his most fervent wishes and his devoutest hopes, it is not to be wondered that he did not reap love, but that the heathens retorted with direst hatred and detestation. Here, too, we will recall to mind the picture which Deutero-Isaiah drew of Israel, where, as the servant of God, it is despised and contemned for the welfare of the earth. That the development of Judaism took this special direction was a necessity of the history of religion.

For the heaviest struggle of Judaism still awaited it; the struggle against Hellenism. One hundred and twenty-five years after Ezra, Alexander the Great destroyed the Persian empire and made the Greeks the sovereign people of the Eastern world. Through this a profound transformation was begun, which spread with startling rapidity and irresistible might, and led finally to the denationalising of the East. That which the Assyrians had undertaken by brute force, the Hellenes surmounted by the superior power of mind and culture. Greece destroyed the nationalities of the East by amalgamating them with itself and conquering them inwardly. Only one Eastern nation withstood the process of dissolution, yea, more, absorbed into itself the good of Hellenism, and thus enriched and strengthened its own existence; and that was the Jewish. If it were able to do this, it was because Ezra and Nehemiah had rendered it hard as steel and strong as iron. In this impenetrable armor it was insured against all attacks, and thus saved religion against Hellenism. And therefore it behooves us to bless the prickly rind, to which alone we owe it, that the noble core remained preserved.

THE LATER PROPHETS.

THE narrow Judaising tendency of Ezra and Nehemiah must have exercised a fatal influence on prophecy, as the issue soon proved. The next prophetic book is that of Joel, which some people in consequence of an almost inconceivable confusion of ideas still declare to be the oldest of all. Few results of Old Testament research are as surely determined and as firmly established as that the Book of Joel dates from the century between Ezra and Alexander the Great.

In Joel for the first time that distinctive note is wanting which in all the older prophetic writings without exception, from Amos to Malachi, was the chief concern of the prophets, namely, censure, constant reference to the sins of Israel. Joel describes Israel as devout and pleasing in the sight of God; all is as it should be. In the regularly and conscientiously conducted ritual of the Temple, Israel has the guarantee of the grace of God; the most beauteous promises are held out to it, while the heathen will be destroyed by God and his angels as the harvest is cut down by the sickle and grapes trampled in the press; and moreover, the Jews shall turn their "ploughshares into swords and their pruning-hooks into spears." The celebrated pouring-out of the spirit will affect only Jewish flesh; the Gentiles shall no longer be considered.

The small Book of Obadiah, written probably at an earlier date, has the same aims; it is the revision of an older prophecy concerning Edom, already known to Jeremiah. To this book are appended the hopes and expectations of the time.

The next great universal catastrophe, however, was to find a more joyful echo in prophecy. This was the destruction of the Persian empire through Alexander the Great. The extremely remarkable coherent fragment, which we now read as Chapters 24 to 27 of the Book of Isaiah, dates, according to sure indications, from this time. We again find in this a reflexion of the old prophetic spirit. The dissolution of the whole earth and the judgment passed upon its inhabitants is the chief theme. But this dissolution is thoroughly justified through the sinfulness of the world, and there, as in Kaulbach's Hunnenschlacht (the battle of the Huns), the decisive struggle takes place, not on earth, but on high. God conquers the host of the high ones; takes them prisoners, and shuts them up for many days in the prison. Israel itself takes no part in the struggle; it merely waits on God as a psalm-singing community, and receives this command:

"Come, my people, enter thou into thy chambers, and shut thy doors about thee; hide thyself for a little moment, until the indignation be overpast. For behold, the Lord cometh forth out of his place to punish the inhabitants of the earth for their iniquity."

The final object of this judgment is the conversion of the earth. Even the imprisoned spirits will be pardoned, when they have lived out the time of their punishment.

"With my soul have I desired thee in the night; yea, with my spirit within me will I seek thee early: for when thy judgments are in the earth, the inhabitants of the world learn righteousness. Let favor be shewed to the wicked, yet will he not learn righteousness: in the land of uprightness will he deal wrongfully, and will not behold the majesty of the Lord."

Then will God prepare on Mount Zion a great feast for all the converted nations and will destroy the face of the covering that is cast over all people and the veil that is spread over all nations, and the kingdom of peace shall begin, whose walls and bulwark are salvation. Only Moab will be excluded from this general salvation, and its destruction is described in revolting imagery—and thus we find again in this usually pure blood a drop of poison.

The most remarkable of all in this fragment is, that the resurrection of the dead here appears for the first time as a postulate of faith, though indeed only the resurrection of the pious Israelites. Now, this postulate, too, takes its origin in the Messianic hypotheses. Among the devout dead is many a martyr, who has suffered death for his God and his faith. Are these, who deserve it before all others, to be excluded from the glory of the kingdom of the Messiah? The justice of God demands that they shall rise again from the dead. Moreover, the living Jews are far too few to become in reality the sovereign and dominant people in the Messianic kingdom; to fill up this want, all the devout Jews who have previously departed must live again. An enlivening dew sent by God shall drop upon these mouldering bones, the dead arise again, and the earth give back the departed spirits.

We find in single sentences of these four chapters much that is beautiful and deep. They show upon the whole a magnificent picture, which shines all the more brightly, when compared with the production which dates next in point of time.

This is the fragment which we now read as Chapters 9 to 14 of the Book of Zechariah. It dates from the beginning of the third century, from the time of the struggles of the Diadochi, when it certainly seemed as if the dominion of the Greeks established by Alexander the Great would fall to pieces. This fragment marks the lowest degradation of the prophetic literature of Israel. The fantasy of the writer positively wades in the blood of the Gentiles; their flesh shall consume away while they stand upon their feet, their eyes shall consume away in their sockets, and their tongues in their mouths, while the sons of Zion, whom God has aroused against the Greeks, will drink their blood like wine and be filled with it like bowls at the corners of the altar. Jerusalem alone shall remain grand and sublime, and even the bells of the horses and every pot shall be holy unto the Lord. The remaining heathen will indeed turn to God, but how shall this conversion show itself? By eating kosher (i. e. after the manner of the Jews) and by going up every year to Jerusalem to keep the feast of tabernacles.

It is impossible to turn the mind of an Amos or a Hosea, of an Isaiah or a Jeremiah, into a worse caricature than is done here. The unknown author of this fragment in the Book of Zechariah will not even be a prophet: we find a very remarkable passage in this fragment, which shows that men distinctly felt that prophecy was at an end, and that the prophetic inspiration in Israel was dying out.

"And it shall come to pass in that day, said the Lord Zebaoth, that I will cut off the names of the idols out of the land, and they shall no more be remembered: and also I will cause the prophets and the unclean spirits to come out of the land. And it shall come to pass, that when any shall yet prophesy, then his father and his mother that begat him shall say unto him: Thou shalt not live, for thou speakest lies in the name of the Lord: and his father and his mother that begat him shall thrust him through when he prophesieth. And it shall come to pass in that day, that the prophets shall be ashamed every one of his vision, when he hath prophesied; neither shall they wear a hairy mantle to deceive: but he shall say, I am no prophet, I am an husbandman; the field is my possession and my trade from my youth up. And if one shall say unto him, What are these wounds thou bearest? he shall answer, . . . I was wounded in the house of my friends."

The prophets deceivers of the people, who must be put to death, prophetic inspiration an unclean spirit, put on the same level with idols—what a change, what a transition! Here we have the whole difference between Israel and Judaism.

Nevertheless the prophetic genius of Israel had not yet utterly died out; it had still sufficient health and strength to enter a strong protest against this caricature of itself, and to pronounce upon it the sentence of its condemnation. This is the special and lasting significance of the little book, which we must look upon as the last of the prophetic literature, the Book of Jonah.

JONAH AND DANIEL.

AN INVOLUNTARY smile passes over one's features at the mention of the name of Jonah. For the popular conception sees nothing in this Book but a silly tale, exciting us to derision. Whenever shallow humor prompts people to hold the Old Testament up to ridicule Balaam's ass and Jonah's whale infallibly take precedence.

I have read the Book of Jonah at least a hundred times, and I will publicly avow, for I am not ashamed of my weakness, that I cannot even now take up this marvellous book, nay, nor even speak of it, without the tears rising to my eyes, and my heart beating higher. This apparently trivial book is one of the deepest and grandest that was ever written, and I should like to say to every one who approaches it, "Take off thy shoes, for the place whereon thou standest is holy ground." In this book Israelitic prophecy quits the scene of battle as victor, and as victor in its severest struggle—that against self. In it the prophecy of Israel succeeded, as Jeremiah expresses it in a remarkable and well-known passage, in freeing the precious from the vile and in finding its better self again.

The Jonah of this book is a prophet, and a genuine representative of the prophecy of the time, a man like unto that second Zechariah, drunk with the blood of the heathen, and who could hardly await the time when God should destroy the whole of the Gentile world. He receives from God the command to go to Nineveh to proclaim the judgment, but he rose to flee from the presence of the Lord by ship unto Tartessus (Tarshish) in the far west. From the very beginning of the narrative the genuine and loyal devotion of the heathen seamen is placed in intentional and exceedingly powerful contrast to the behavior of the prophet; they are the sincere believers; he is the only heathen on board. After that Jonah has been saved from storm and sea by the fish, he again receives the command to go to Nineveh. He obeys, and wonderful to relate, scarcely has the strange preacher traversed the third part of the city crying out his warning than the whole of Nineveh proclaimed a fast and put on sackcloth; the people of Nineveh believed the words of the preacher and humiliated themselves before God. Therefore, the ground and motive of the divine judgment ceased to exist: "God repented of the evil that He thought to do them, and He did it not." Now comes the fourth chapter, on account of which the whole book was written, and which I cannot refrain from repeating word for word, as its simple and ingenuous mode of narration belongs essentially to the attainment of that mood which is so stirring to the heart, and cannot be replaced by paraphrase.

"Now this (God's determining not to destroy Nineveh because of its sincere repentance) displeased Jonah exceedingly and he was very angry. And he prayed unto the Lord and said, I pray thee, O Lord, was not this my saying, when I was yet in my country? Therefore I hasted to flee unto Tarshish: for I knew that thou art a gracious God, and full of compassion, slow to anger, and plenteous in mercy, and repentest thee of the evil. Therefore, now, O Lord, take, I beseech thee, my life from me; for it is better for me to die than to live. Then said the Lord, Doest thou well to be angry? Then Jonah went out of the city, and sat on the east side of the city, and there made him a booth, and sat under it in the shadow, till he might see what would become of the city. And the Lord God prepared a gourd and made it to come up over Jonah, that it might be a shadow over his head. And Jonah was exceedingly glad of the gourd. But God prepared a worm when the morning rose the next day, and it smote the gourd that it withered. And it came to pass, when the sun did arise, that God prepared a sultry east wind; and the sun beat upon the head of Jonah that he grew faint, and requested for himself that he might die, and said, It is better for me to die than to live. And God said to Jonah, Doest thou well to be angry for the gourd? And he said, I do well to be angry even unto death. Then said the Lord, Thou hast had pity on the gourd, for the which thou hast not labored, neither madest it grow; which came up in a night and perished in a night. And should not I have pity on Nineveh, that great city, wherein are more than six score thousand persons that cannot discern between their right hand and their left hand; and also much cattle?"

With this question closes the last book of the prophetic literature of Israel. More simply, as something quite self-evident, and therefore more sublimely and touchingly, the truth was never spoken in the Old Testament, that God, as Creator of the whole earth, must also be the God and father of the entire world, in whose loving, kind, and fatherly heart all men are equal, before whom there is no difference of nation and confession, but only men, whom He has created in his own image. Here Hosea and Jeremiah live anew. The unknown author of the Book of Jonah stretches forth his hand to these master hearts and intellects. In the celestial harmony of the infinite Godly love and of the infinite Godly pity, the Israelitic prophecy rings out as the most costly bequest of Israel to the whole world.

I have spoken as if with the Book of Jonah the prophetic literature of Israel had come to an end, and occasioned thereby no doubt considerable surprise. For up to the present no mention has been made of a book which ranks among the best known, or, to speak more accurately, among those of whose existence we know something—namely, the Book of Daniel. Daniel in the den of the lions, the three men in the fiery furnace, the feast of Belshazzar with the Mene Tekel, the colossus with the feet of clay, are all well known, and have become, so to speak, household words. Surely, the reception of such a book into the prophetic literature cannot be disputed! Yet I must remark that according to the Jewish canon this book is never reckoned among the prophetic writings. This was first done by the Greek Bible, and thus it became the custom throughout the whole Christian Church to designate Daniel together with Isaiah, Jeremiah, and Ezekiel as the four great prophets, in contradistinction to the so-called twelve minor prophets.

It would take me too long to explain the reasons which induced the Synagogue to enter upon this apparently strange proceeding. However, I cannot withdraw from my plain duty of including the Book of Daniel in my comments upon the Israelitic prophecies. And it well deserves consideration; for it is one of the most important and momentous that was ever written. We still work with conceptions and employ expressions which are derived immediately from the Book of Daniel. The entire hierarchy of heaven, with the four archangels, the doctrine of the resurrection of the dead, the idea of a kingdom of heaven, the designation of the Messianic ruler in this kingdom as the Son of Man, are found mentioned for the first time in the Book of

Daniel. The Book of Daniel dates from the last great crisis in the history of the religion of the Old Testament, and the most important and difficult of all—its life-and-death struggle with Hellenism.

In the year 333 B. C., through the great victory at Issus, the whole of Asia Minor had fallen into the hands of Alexander the Great, who thereupon immediately turned his attention to the conquest of Syria, Phœnicia, and Palestine. Thus Judæa came under the Grecian sway. When, in the year 323, Alexander died, at the age of thirty-four, the long struggles and strife of the Diadochi ensued, who fought for the inheritance of the dead monarch. The battle of Ipsus, 301, put an end to these dissensions. Out of the great universal empire founded by Alexander four Hellenistic kingdoms arose: Macedonia, the parent country, which was lost to the house of Alexander after unspeakable atrocities, the Pergamenian kingdom of the Attalidæ, the Syrian kingdom of the Seleucidæ, and the Egyptian of the Ptolemies.

Judæa and Coelesyria were annexed to the kingdom of the Ptolemies, and remained an Egyptian province for over a hundred years. And the first half of this period, outwardly viewed, was the happiest that Judæa had experienced since the loss of its independence. The three first Ptolemies were powerful and talented rulers, who were extremely prepossessed in favor of the Jews and supported and encouraged them in every way, because, as Josephus tells us, the Jews were the only people on whose oath they could implicitly rely; what a Jew had once sworn he abided by without deviation.

Soon, however, the complications of war arose. The Seleucidæ stretched out their hands covetously towards the province of Egypt, and after varying conflicts it was finally incorporated in the year 198 in the kingdom of Syria. At first the Jews seemed to have hailed the new government with delight, but the Syrian domination was soon to show itself in all its terribleness. Antiochus IV., Epiphanes, a man of violent temper and limited ideas, was anxious to accelerate by violence the process of Hellenising, which was already going on satisfactorily, and set himself the task of totally eradicating, by the police power of the State, the Jewish nationality and the Jewish religion. Then began that terrible persecution of the orthodox Jews, which the Book of Maccabees describes on the whole correctly, though with some exaggerations. Antiochus, however, only aided thereby the holy cause against which he fought; he shook the righteous from their slumbers, forced the wavering to decision, and thus gave to Judaism the last blow of the hammer which was to weld that which Ezra and Nehemiah perhaps had not sufficiently forged.

From this date Judaism appears to us as Pharisaism. Who knows whether without this violent interference matters would not have taken a different course? We know by unequivocal evidence that Hellenism had already made vast strides, that especially the cultured and aristocratic circles, and even the priesthood, were completely under its influence.

But this brutal attack aroused the opposition of despair. The Jewish people carried on the struggle thus forced upon them with almost superhuman efforts. The mightiest Greek armies fled in dismay before the frenzied courage of these men battling for what was most sacred to them; and they finally succeeded in shaking off the heathen rule, and in once again founding a national Jewish State under the house of the Maccabees.

In the fiercest moments of this contest, in January, 164, we know the very day almost, the Book of Daniel was written, in which the clear flame of the first holy inspiration still burns. When we picture to ourselves the unspeakable sufferings of the Jewish nation, we can only wonder with reverent admiration at the unknown author of the Book of Daniel, who knew how to keep himself clean from all the baser human national passions, and only to give enthusiastic expression to the final victory of the cause of God. There is the difference of day and night between the Book of Daniel and that of Esther, written but a generation later. As in Jonah, so in Daniel Israelitic prophecy flared upwards like a bright flame for the last time, to die in a manner worthy of its grand and magnificent past.

We have now reached the end of our task. We have followed the prophecies of Israel from their beginning to their close, and I should be glad if I have succeeded in producing upon my readers the impression that we have been treating here of the organic development of one of the greatest spiritual forces that the history of man has ever witnessed, and of the most important and most magnificent section of the history of religion previously to Christ. If Israel became in the matter of religion the chosen people of the whole world, it owes this to prophecy, which first clearly conceived the idea of a universal religion, and established it in all its foundations. Prophecy lived again in John the Baptist. And Jesus of Nazareth in contrast to the pharisaical Judaism of his time purposely links his own activity to the prophecy of ancient Israel, himself its purest blossom and noblest fruit. Jewish prophecy is Mary, the mother of Christianity, and the Christian church has known no better designation for the earthly pilgrimage of its founder than to speak of him in his office as prophet. As far as the influence of Christianity extends, so far also the effects of the Israelitic prophecy reach, and when the oldest of the literary prophets, Amos, speaks of prophecy as the noblest gift of grace, which God gave to Israel and only to Israel, a history of two thousand five hundred years has but justified his assertion.

The whole history of humanity has produced nothing which can be compared in the remotest degree to the prophecy of Israel. Through prophecy Israel became the prophet of mankind. Let this never be overlooked nor forgotten: the costliest and noblest treasure that man possesses he owes to Israel and to Israelitic prophecy.

INDEX.

Aaron, Moses's prophet, 10.

Abiathar, high-priest of David, banished by Solomon, probable ancestor of Jeremiah, 92.

Abraham, a historical character, 16; his religion, 18.

Admah, Shall I make thee as, 52.

Ahab, king of Israel, his conflict with Elijah, character and rule, 29-33; his prophets, 13-30.

Ahajiah, son of Ahab and Jezebel, 30.

Ahaz, king of Judah, character, 61-62; the voluntary vassal of Tiglath-Pileser, 63; his political foresight and death, 64.

Abijah, of Shiloh, prophet, 28.

Ahikam, father of Gedaliah, 106.

Ahura-Mazda, religion of the Persians, 145.

Alexander the Great, attempts to Hellenise the Orient, 162-163; his destruction of the Persian empire calls forth chapters 24-27 of the Book of Isaiah, 165; his conquest of the Orient including Judæa, 175; his death, 175.

Amasis, king of Egypt, opposes Persia, 146.

Amaziah, priest, repels Amos, 41.

Amon, king of Judah, 80.

Amos, disclaims being a prophet of the old type, 14, 41; on the mission and character of prophecy, 35, 178; personality and achievements, 37-46; reconciliatory conclusion of his book, 47, 111.

Anathoth, Jeremiah's birthplace, 92.

Angels, employed by Zechariah as intermediaries between the prophets and God, 152-153.

Animal-worship, 18, 37, 52.

Anointed of God, Cyrus the, 135.

Antiochus IV., Epiphanes, attempts to Hellenise the Jews by force, but is repulsed, 176-177.

Apocalyptical riders, in Zechariah, 153.

Arabic, importance of, for Hebrew etymology, 9-12.

Arabs, obliterate their history, 3.

Aramaic nationality, eradicated by the Assyrians, 109.

Archangels, the four, derived from Daniel, 174.

Artaxerxes (Longimanus), Persian king, permits the reforms of Ezra, 160.

Aryans, their early civilisation, 6 et seq.

Asp, The sucking child shall play on the hole of the, 60.

Asshur be their king, 51.

Assyrians, threaten Israel, 29, 42; Isaiah's view of their divine mission, 57, 64-66; in the zenith of their glory, 72, 76; their oppressive rule, 73; their customs and forms of worship introduced into Judæa, 74 75; their decline and downfall, 76, 78, 79, 99-101; Habakkuk's description of, 78; their use of the exile, 108.

Astarte, Phœnician goddess, 23.

Astyages, king of the Medes, conquered by Cyrus, 129.

Asurbanipal, Assyrian king, 72; his

wars in Egypt, Arabia, and Syria, 73.
Athaljah, daughter of Jezebel and Ahab, 30.
Attalidæ, kingdom of, 175.

Baal, prophets of, 13; proper interpretation of Ahab's worship of, 30; opposed by Elijah, 31; extirpated from Samaria, 33; forms and influence of his worship among the Jews, 49, 81, 118, 127.
Baalim, They sacrificed unto, 51.
Babylon, city, its grandeur, 112; its fall, 144.
Babylonian exile. See *Exile, the Babylonian*.
Babylonians, religion of, 22-23, 26; their history and fall, 128-130, 156.
Backsliding, My people are bent to, 52.
Balaam, his talking ass, 170.
Balance, weigh the hills in a, 136.
Beersheba, place of worship, 26.
Bells, of horses, holy, 168.
Belshazzar, the feast of, 174.
Berosus, Babylonian historian, 129.
Beside Me, no God, 138.
Bethel, place of worship, Amos at the Autumn festival of, 37 et seq.; also 26, 52.
Bird of passage, 97.
Blemished thing, sacrifice not a, 157.
Blind offerings, 157.
Bowels, my, 95.
Brotherly love, emphasised by Ezekiel, 121.
Bull, ancient symbol of the God of Israel, 37, 52.

Calves, the golden, of Dan and Bethel, 126-127; Hosea's name for the bull-symbols of God, 52.
Calvin, Ezekiel compared to, 116.
Cambyses III., king of Persia, subdues Egypt, commits suicide, 149.
Canaanites, character of the prophets of, 13; child-sacrifice and religious unchastity of, 18, 23; forms and places of Israelitic worship borrowed from, 26; their language adopted by the Israelites, 18.
Caphtor, Have I not brought the Philistines from, 43.
Captivity of the ten tribes of Israel, 69, 109. See *Exile, the Babylonian*.
Carchemish, battle of, 101.
Chaldeans, predicted by Habakkuk as the destroyers of the Assyrians, 78; take Nineveh and defeat the Egyptians, 101; their divine mission, 104; period of their rule, 127-128, 145. See *Babylonians*.
Charles the Great, his love of pagan literature, 3.
Cherubs, meaning of, 21.
Child-sacrifice in Canaan, 18; in Judæa, 74, 75.
Christ, erroneous view of prophecy's relation to, 5. See *Jesus*.
Christianity, its relation to prophecy, 178.
Church and state, the opposition of, created by Deuteronomy, 88-89, 114.
Circumcision of the heart, Jeremiah's, 97, 98; becomes circumcision of the flesh in Deutero-Isaiah, 143.
Clergy, distinguished from the laity, 87.
Cockatrice' den, the weaned child shall put his hand on, 60.
Coelesyria, annexed by the Ptolemies, 175.
Colossus, with the feet of clay, 174.
Come, my people, enter thou, 166.
Comfort ye, my people, 132.
Commandments, the Ten, when written, 17.
Congregation, religious, Ezekiel's idea of a, 120.
Copernicus, 4.
Cords of a man, with, 51.
Covenant of grace, God's, with Israel, 106.
Cultus. See *Worship*.
Cuneiform inscriptions, 147.
Cyrus, conquers the Medes and founds the Persian empire, 129-130; named the executor of God's judgment on Babylon, God's shepherd and anointed, by Deutero-Isaiah,

133-135, 139; takes Babylon and grants the Jews permission to return to Jerusalem, 144-145; reasons for helping the Jews, religious liberalism, etc., 144-147.

Damascus, its struggle with Israel, 29, 39; made an Assyrian province, 63.

Dan, place of worship, 26, 52.

Daniel, Book of, not reckoned among the prophetic writings by the Jewish canon, 174; its origin, character, and significance, 174-177.

Dante, 2.

Darius, Persian emperor, kills the Magus Gaumata, reorganises and consolidates the Persian empire, 149-150, 154.

Daughter, meaning of, 7.

David, House of, its rôle in the Messianic schemes, 59, 72, 75, 126. See *Messiah*.

Day of wrath, etc., 77.

Dead letter, substituted for the living revelation by Deuteronomy, 89.

Deborah, prophetess, song of, oldest production of Israelitic literature, 20, 27.

Delphi, the oracle at, 11.

Destroy, I cannot come to, 52.

Deutero-Isaiah (= Chaps. 40-66 of the canonical book of Isaiah), also called *Isaiah, the Second*, which see.

Deuteronomy, its promulgation, 81-83; its conceptions and aims, 83 et seq.; its reform of the cultus, 83-87; its establishment of a professional priesthood, 87-88; its creation of the opposition of church and state, 88; its introduction of externalism in worship, 89; its tremendous importance, 82, 89-90; made the fundamental law of the kingdom, 82; its ideas receive their fullest development in the Babylonian exile, 113; saves Israel and religion, 107; its ideas followed by Ezekiel, 122; creates book-religion, 152; its ultimate conclusions drawn by the Babylonian Jews, 159, 161.

De Wette, his Old Testament researches, 82-83, 111.

Diadochi, successors of Alexander the Great, the struggles of, as influencing prophecy and the Jews, 167, 175.

Dies iræ, dies illa, taken from Zephaniah, 76, 77.

Dirge, Israel's funeral, used by Amos at the festival of Bethel, 40.

Divina Comedia, 2.

Dodona, oracle at, 11.

Drunken women, at the Israelitic festivals, 38.

Dschebel Oscha, Mount Hosea, 55.

Dürer, Albrecht, 126.

Dust to his sword, as, 134.

Ecbatana, capital of Media, 129.

Edom, prophecy concerning, 165.

Edomite king, burnt by the Moabites, 46.

Egypt, Abraham in, 16; its struggle with Assyria, 65-67, 73, 76; aids the Jews against Nebuchadnezzar, 104; under Amasis, opposes Persia, 146; subdued by Cambyses, 149; under the Ptolemies and the Seleucidæ, 175-176; religion of, 22, 44.

El, Semitic word for God, 7.

Eli, reproves the mother of Samuel, 38.

Elijah, prophet, not a native of Palestine, 12; ecstatic traits in, 13-14; makes a pilgrimage to Horeb, 20; his historical import and achievements, 29, 36; the first truly Israelitic prophet, 34, 126; subsequently regarded as the forerunner and pioneer of the Messianic kingdom, 158.

Elisha, prophet, has Jehu anointed king, 13; arouses the prophetic inspiration by means of music, 14; his relation to Elijah and character, 33.

Eloquent, I am not, etc., 10.

Ephraim, I taught, also to walk, 51; How shall I give thee up? 52.

Equity, that pervert all, 70.

Esarhaddon, Assyrian king, conquers Egypt, 72, 73.

Es-Salt, 55.
Esther, the Book of, 177.
Ethbaal, Jezebel's father, 30.
Ethiopians, are ye not as the children of, 43.
Etymology, significance for historical research, 6 et seq.
Euphrates, 39, 110.
Evil, hate the, 43.
Evil Merodach, Babylonian king, 129.
Exile, first used by the Assyrians as a means of pacifying rebellious tribes, 108 et seq.
Exile, the Babylonian, 106; its religious consequences, 110 et seq.; its moral influences, 112; its realisation of Deuteronomic ideas, 113; creates Judaism, 114; the literary work of, consists of the compilation of the historical traditions of Israel and of the establishment of a theodicy, 125-128; intellectual and material condition of the Jews during, 125-128; the return from, 144-149; religious condition of the Jews in the period succeeding, 155 et seq.
Exodus, quotation from, 10.
Externalism, religious, introduced by Deuteronomy, 89.
Eyes, consume in their sockets, 167.
Ezekiel, prophet, son of Buzi, the first dogmatist and theologian of the Old Testament, 114, 117; his early activity, 115; his character, 116-117; his leading ideas, 117 et seq.; his vindication of God, 118, 126; his pastoral care of souls and theory of the prophetic office, 119-120; makes the Sabbath the fundamental institution of Judaism, 120-121; emphasises the virtue of chastity, 121; his description of the Kingdom of God and of the new Jerusalem, 121-124; founds the theocracy of the Jews, 123-124; his ideas worked out by the Babylonian Jews, 159.
Ezra, reformer and founder of Judaism, 160-163.

Family life, its purity emphasised by Ezekiel, 121.
Fat, make the heart of this people, 61.
Faust, 2.
Feasts, old Israelitic, 23; their character, 37-39; borrowed from the Canaanites, 26; their transformation by Deuteronomy, 85-87.
Filth, Isaiah applies this term to the Jewish forms of worship, 72.
Fishes of the sea, treateth men as, 78.
Flax, smoking, shall he not quench, 142.
Flower of the field, as the, 133.
Folly, era of, pre-Islamitic, 3.
Forgive, I can no longer, 44.
Fowler, the snares of the, 54.
Frederick Barbarossa, 126.
Fundamental writing (*Grundschrift*) of the Pentateuch, written in Babylon, the foundation of the reform of Ezra, 159-160.
Funeral dirge, has a special poetical form in ancient Israel, 41.

Gad, prophet, 28.
Gaumata, the Magus, usurps the throne of Cambyses, slain by Darius, 149-150.
Gedaliah, first Babylonian viceroy of Judah, slain by a band of fanatics, 106.
Genesis, child-sacrifice in, 18.
Gentiles, referred to, 118, 120, 135; their relations to the Jews, 98, 143; their power flourishes unabated, 156; shall be destroyed by God, 167, 168, 171. See also the proper names of the various heathen nations.
Germans, their destruction of their pagan literature, 3; delve into the poetic treasures of their past, 126.
God, etymology of the Hebrew word for, 19 et seq.; Elijah's conception of, 31; idea of, in Amos, 42, 47; in Hosea, 47, 52; in Isaiah, 57, 66; in Ezekiel, 116-118; in the Second Isaiah, 135 et seq., 140 et seq.; in Jonah, 171-173; ancient Israel's conception of, 24 et seq., 27, 37 et

seq., 83, 85; Deuteronomy's conception of, 84; the prophetic conception of, 84, 94-95; the struggles of the God of the people with the God of the prophets, 72, 111-112; his omnipotence emphasised by Deutero-Isaiah, 135 et seq,; his exclusive divinity proclaimed by Deutero-Isaiah, 136-139; his supposed abandonment of his people after the exile, 155 et seq.; his arraignment and justification in the post-exilic period, 158.

God-belief of the Israelites compared with the religion of the Persians, 145.

Goddess, feminine form does not exist in Hebrew, 23.

Gog of Magog, Ezekiel's, 123.

Goldsmith, makes idols, 136-137.

Gourd, Jonah's, 172.

Gibeon, place of worship, 26.

Gilgal, place of worship, 26.

Grass, all flesh is, 133.

Grasshoppers, inhab. of earth as, 136.

Greek Bible, admits Daniel as one of the major prophets, 174.

Greek Catholic chapel at Wiesbaden, 30.

Greeks, their intellectual conquest of the Orient, 162-163; struggle of the Jews against, 175-177.

Gregory VII., Ezekiel compared to, 116.

Grundschrift, of the Pentateuch, 159-160.

Habakkuk, prophet, 78-79.

Haggai, prophet, 150-152.

Hājāh, Hebrew word, to be, 19.

Halt, how long will ye, between two opinions, 31.

Hamath, in Syria, 149.

Hananiah, false prophet, opponent of Jeremiah, 103.

Händel, his *Messiah*, 132.

Haran, in Mesopotamia, 16.

Harlot, thy wife shall be an, 41.

Hawâ, Arabic verb, to fall, 20.

Hellenism. See *Greeks*.

Henotheism, 24.

Henry the Fowler, 126.

Herbs, like a clear heat on, 66.

Herdman, But I was an, 14, 41.

Hermes, 9.

Hewâ, Aramaic verb, to be, 19.

Hezekiah, king of Judah, revolts against his Assyrian suzerain, 64 et seq.; his reforms of the worship, 68, 71, 74.

Hierarchy of heaven, The, derived from Daniel, 174.

Hilkiah, priest, delivers Deuteronomy to Josiah's scribe, 81.

Historical works of the Jews, compiled during the exile, 125-128.

Horeb, or Sinai, 20.

Hosea, censures the bloody deeds of Jehu, 33; his history, character, and achievements, 49-55; his conception of God, 47-48; his domestic troubles typical of his religious activity, 48-49; his view of God's relation to Israel, 49-50; his God a God of love, 50-52; his fervor and subjectivity, 51; repudiates paganism and idolatry, 52; founds the faith and theology of Israel, 53; his portrayal of his time, 53; creates the theocracy of the Old Testament, 54; his personal martyrdom, 54; compared with Isaiah, 69; attributes the decay of Israel to the paganism of its worship, 71; contrasted with Jeremiah, 91-92; on the threatened exile, 109, 127; Jonah compared with, 173.

Hosts, Lord of. See *Zebaoth*.

Huldah, prophetess, declares in favor of Deuteronomy, 82.

Humbly, walk, with thy God, 76.

Hunnenschlacht, of Kaulbach, 165.

Hybris, the Greek, 79.

Idolatry, of Ahab and Solomon, 30 et seq.; satirised by Deutero-Isaiah, 136 et seq.

Incense, introduced into Judæa, 74.

Individualism, religious, in Jeremiah and Ezekiel, 120.

Indo-Europeans, early civilisation of, 6 et seq.

Inspiration, divine, idea of, introduced by Deuteronomy, 90.

Ipsus, battle of, 175.

Isaac, intended sacrifice of, its religio-historical meaning, 18.

Isaiah, compares prophecy to a sealed book, 1; mentions the seraphs, 21; describes the revels in the temple at Jerusalem, 38; his rank and practical character, 56; his conception of God and His omnipotence, 57; his conception of universal history, 57; his idea of the "remnant" and "holy seed," 58 et seq.; his conception of the future kingdom of God, 59 et seq.; his invocation of the judgment, 61; seeks to dictate the policy of Ahaz, 62; devotes his energies to the education of the remnant, 63; his view of the Assyrian's divine rôle, 64-67; his theory of the inviolability of Mt. Zion, 65-67, 75, 84, 103-104; the motive power in Hezekiah's reform, 68; his death, influence, and character, 68-69; opposed by Micah, 70; attributes the decay of Israel to the paganism of its worship, 71; satirises the Jewish forms of worship, 72; the attitude of Judah towards his reforms, 72; compared with Ezekiel, 116.

Isaiah, the Second (also called Deutero-Isaiah), his work embraces Chapters 40-66 of the canonical Book of Isaiah, 131; flourishes during the Babylonian captivity, 130-131; personality and character, 131-132, 143; despite his brilliancy begins the decline of prophecy, 132, 143; foretells the deliverance of the Jews, 132-135, 144; names Cyrus the shepherd and anointed of God, 135; his constant emphasis of the omnipotence of God, 135 et seq.; satirises the idols of the heathen, 136 et seq.; on monotheism, 136 et seq.; his gorgeous pictures of the new Jerusalem, 139, 155; his view of Israel as the prophet and servant of God to the whole earth, 140-143, 162; compared with Jeremiah, 143; marks the separation of Judaism from Israelitism, 143.

Isaiah, Chapters 24-27, written in the time of Alexander the Great, 165; an indication of the revival of the prophetic spirit, 167; first makes the resurrection of the dead a postulate of faith, 166-167.

Islam, 3.

Israel, study of its history, 2-4; oldest historical traditions of, 16 et seq.; its pre-Mosaic religion, 18; salient points of its religion and ethics before the prophets, 22 et seq.; made into a nation by Moses, 25-26; character of its primitive divine worship, 38 et seq.; Elijah's conception of its mission, 34; Amos predicts its downfall, 44; its religion universalised by Amos, 45; its theology grows out of Hosea, 53; condition of, in the time of Hosea, 53-54; converted into an Assyrian province, 63; captivity of, 69, 109; God's prophet, servant and messenger to the world, 141 et seq., 162, 178-179.

Issus, the battle of, 175.

Jacob, declare unto, his transgression, 36; sees the angels of God, 37; as a maggot, 112, 141.

Jahwe. See *Yahveh*.

Jehoahaz, king of Israel, 33.

Jehoiachin, king of Judah, son of Jehoiakim, capitulates to Nebuchadnezzar and is led captive to Babylon, 102, 115.

Jehoiakim, king of Judah, persecutes the prophets, 100; burns Jeremiah's book of prophecy, 102; converted from an Assyrian into a Babylonian vassal, 102; revolts against Nebuchadnezzar, his death, 102.

Jehoram, son of Ahab and Jezebel, 30.

Jehovah. See *Yahveh*.

Jehu, anointed king, 13; smites the house of Ahab, 33.

Jeremiah, handicapped by Isaiah's

ideas, 68; on Manasseh's persecution of the prophets, 74; prophecy's noblest offshoot and highest culmination, 91, 131-132, 143; not connected with Deuteronomy, 91; contrasted with Hosea, 48, 50, 91-92; his life, call, and wonderful endowments, 92, 93; his conception of his office and of his relation to God, 93-94; his human shortcomings, 94-95; his love for his people, 95-96; his spiritualisation and broadening of religion, 96-99; details of his activity and achievements, 99-106; his sufferings and death, 106-107; his noble and undaunted character, 107; the predecessor of Ezekiel, 117, 120; charged with preaching an impotent God, 118; fixes the period of the Babylonian exile, 110, 127; his circumcision of the heart, 143; compared with Deutero-Isaiah, 140, 143, with Jonah, 173; prophecy concerning Edom, 165.

Jeroboam II., king of Israel, splendor of his reign, 39; the sins of, cause the destruction of Jerusalem, 126-127.

Jerusalem, besieged by Rezin of Damascus and Pekah of Israel, 62; besieged by Sennacherib, 67; besieged by Nebuchadnezzar, 104; taken by Nebuchadnezzar, 105; rebuilt under Cyrus, 146, 148; distressed condition of the new city, 156; centralisation of religious worship in, 84-88; compared with Babylon, 112; destruction of, predicted by Ezekiel, 115; compared to a rusty pot, 118.

Jerusalem, The New, the vision of, in Ezekiel, 122-124; its glories depicted by Deutero-Isaiah, 139, 143, 155.

Jeshua. See *Joshua*.

Jesse, sprig out of the stem of, 60.

Jesus, his work entirely personal, 34; his solution of the religious problem, 84; consciously links his activity to that of the ancient Israelitic prophets, 178. See *Christ*.

Jews, their life during the Babylonian exile, 112-113, 125-130; Deutero-Isaiah's conception of their relation to the Gentiles, 143; liberated by Cyrus, 144-146; their return from the exile, 144-149; physical and mental condition after their return, 147-149, 153-155; their disappointment and lack of faith after the exile, 156; their neglect of their religious duties, 157; character and achievements of those who remained behind in Babylon: draw the last conclusion of Deuteronomy and write the juridical parts of the first book of the Pentateuch, 159; return to Jerusalem and begin the reform known as Judaism, 160-161; withstand the Hellenisation of the Orient, but incur by their exclusiveness the hatred and contempt of all the nations, 161-163; under the Ptolemies, 175; repulse the attempt of Antiochus IV. to Hellenise them, 176; found a new Jewish national state under the Maccabees, 177; the holiness of their oath, 176. See *Jerusalem, Israel*, etc.

Jezebel, Ahab's wife, 30-33.

Jezreel, 14.

Joel, date of his book, represents the degeneracy of prophecy, 154.

John the Baptist, prophecy lives again in, 178.

Jonah, popular misconception of, 170; the significance and touching character of his work, 169-170, 173; rebuked by God, 172-173; compared with Hosea and Jeremiah, 173.

Josephus, coins the word "theocracy," 124; on the oath of the Jews, 175-176.

Joshua (= Jeshua), priest, minister of the returned exiles, 148; high-priest, 149; assists in rebuilding the second temple, 151.

Josiah, king of Judah, his accession to the throne, 80; his influence won by the prophetic party, 81; proclaims Deuteronomy as the fundamental law of the kingdom, 82, 161;

his reforms of the worship, 83, 90, 127; slain at the battle of Megiddo, 100; character and achievements, 99, 117-118.

Judæa, the natural port of entry from Asia to Africa, 73, 146; annexed to the kingdom of the Ptolemies, 175; conquered by the Seleucidæ, 176; independent under the house of the Maccabees, 177.

Judah, succeeds Israel, 56; critical period of its history, 56, 62-68; the "legitimacy" of its government, 59; saved by Ahaz's policy, 64; invaded by Sennacherib, 67; under the Assyrians, 72-73; destroyed as a nation, and transformed into a church by the Babylonian exile, 113-114.

Judaism, as contradistinguished from Israelitism, created by the Babylonian exile, 110, 113-114; initiated by Deutero-Isaiah, 143; definitively established by Ezra and Nehemiah, its character and influence, 161-164; contrasted with the old Israelitic ideas, 169; transformed into Pharisaism, 176.

Judgment, let, run down as waters; establish, in the gate, 43.

Judgment, the divine, its function, 127; the post-exilic, predicted by Malachi, 158. See the different prophets.

Justice, as the cardinal attribute of God, in Amos, 45-47; turned to wormwood, 44.

Kalchas, soothsayer, 5.
Karmel, 14.
Kaulbach's *Hunnenschlacht*, 165.
Kindness, my, shall not depart from thee, 139.
King, a counsellor, in Semitic, 7; I am a great, saith the Lord, 158.
Kingdom of God, Isaiah's conception of, 59-61; in Deuteronomy, 83; Ezekiel's description of, 121-124; expected after the exile, 153-154; the idea of, in Daniel, 174.
Kings, Book of, referred to, 23, 53.

Kir, Have I not brought up the Syrians from, 43.
Kishon, battle of, 20.
Kôhen, Hebrew, for priest, 8.
Kosher, its meaning, 168.

Labasi-Marduk, king of Babylon, 129.
Laity, first distinguished from the clergy, 87.
Lame in both legs, like a man, 31.
Language, science of, as a help in history, 6 et seq
Lebanon, in the glory and scent of, 50; not sufficient to burn, 136.
Lees, settled on their, 81.
Legalism, the doctrine of, in Judaism, 159.
Leopard, and the kid, 60.
Levi, the tribe of, 16, 87.
Levites, 122.
Leviticus, written by the post-exilic Babylonian Jews, 159-160.
Lies, our fathers have inherited, 98.
Light, Persian worship of, 145.
Lion, the, hath roared, 35.
Lion's den, Daniel in the, 174.
Longhand. See *Artaxerxes*.
Lord of Hosts. See *Zebaoth*.
Lord, thy God, the, a phrase coined by Hosea, 52.
Love, as an attribute of God in Hosea, 47-48; in Jonah, 173; brotherly, emphasised by Ezekiel, 121.
Lydia, conquered by Cyrus, 129.

Maccabees, their rebellion and foundation of an independent Jewish state, 176-177; their state destroyed by the idea of theocracy, 124.
Macedonia, 175.
Mad, the spiritual man is, 54.
Maggot, Jacob as a, 112, 141.
Magog, in Ezekiel's vision, 123.
Major prophets, 174.
Malachi, prophet, leader of the devout remnant, 156-159.
Manasseh, king of Judah, 73; his persecution of the prophets, and his idolatry, 74-75, 93; his sins cause the destruction of Judah and Jerusalem, 75, 77, 127; his death, 80.

μάντις, Greek for soothsayer, 5.
Marshal, its etymology, 8.
Mary, as the mother of Christianity, Jewish prophecy compared to, 178.
Mazda-Yasnian, Cyrus a, 145.
Medes, attack Assyria and take Nineveh, 76-78, 101; conquered by the Persians, 129.
Mediterranean Sea, 29.
Megiddo, the battle of, 100.
Melek, Semitic word for king, 7.
Mene Tekel, the, 174.
Mercury, 9.
Mercy, how long wilt thou not have, 153; God, plenteous in, 172.
Merodach, Babylonian God, 147.
Mesopotamia, 16, 110.
Messiah, Händel's, 132.
Messianic King, first expected by Isaiah, 59-61; the idea of, in Ezekiel, 119, 122-123; not mentioned by Deutero-Isaiah, 135; Zerubbabel proclaimed as such by Haggai, 155, and by Zechariah, 152, 154; Messianic hope, Kingdom, etc., 159, 167.
Micah, prophet, 69-70; on true and false prophets, 35.
Micah, Chaps. 6-7, 75-76.
Midas, 14.
Milker, Aryan meaning of daughter, 7.
Minor prophets, 174.
Miracles of Elijah, 31-33; of Elisha, 33.
Mizpah, residence of Babylonian viceroy, 106.
Moab, excluded from the general salvation of Isaiah, Chapters 24-27, 166.
Moabites, burn an Edomite king, 46.
Moloch, sacrifices to, 75; worship of, 81.
Monolatry, oldest form of Israelitic God-worship, 24.
Monotheism, did not exist in ancient Israel, 24, 45; first distinctly enunciated by Jeremiah, 97-98.
Moral law, Amos the incorporation of the, 42; demands the destruction of the Assyrians, 79.
Mosaism, date of its origin, 159-160.
Moses, of the tribe of Levi, 16; makes Aaron his "prophet," 10;
character of the traditions concerning, 17; their historical value, 17 et seq.; his religion, 18 et seq.; indirect proof of his work, 22 et seq.; his achievements, 23 et seq.; the forerunner of the prophets, 36; also 72, 126.
Mount Hosea, 55.
Mouth of God, 11.
Müller, Max, 24.

Naba'a, Semitic root, 8-10.
Nābî, the Hebrew word for prophet, 8-13.
Nabopolassar, 9.
Naboth, the Jezreelite, judicial murder of, by Ahab and Jezebel, 31 et seq.
Nabu, Babylonian god, 9.
Nabu-nahid, or Nabonidus, Babylonian king, 129.
Nahum, prophet, 77-79.
Napoleon, 126.
Nassau, Duke of, his Greek Catholic chapel at Wiesbaden, 30.
Nathan, prophet, 28.
Nationality, its roots, 108-109.
Nebālāh, madness, 24.
Nebo, Babylonian god, 9, 147.
Nebuchadnezzar, Babylonian king, takes Nineveh, 101; defeats Necho at Carchemish, 101; viewed by Jeremiah as the weapon of God, 102; defeats and takes captive Jehoiachin, 102; takes Jerusalem and leads the Jews into captivity, 105-106; his towering personality and character, 128-129; origin of his name, 9.
Necho, Egyptian king, defeats Josiah at Megiddo, 100; defeated at Carchemish by Nebuchadnezzar, 101.
Nehemiah, Persian governor of Judæa, associate of Ezra and co-founder of Judaism, 160-163.
Nergalsharezer, king of Babylon, 129.
New moons, feast of, 23.
Nile, 39.
Nineveh, attacked by the Medes, 77-78; its fall, 100-101; Jonah proclaims the judgment on, 171 et seq.; saved by God, 172-173.

Oath, of the Jews, in Hellenistic times, 176.
Obadiah, prophet, 165.
Old Testament history and research, 1, 3, 4, 6.
Old Testament, Spinoza on, 125.
Omri, the dynasty of, 33.
Oracle, ancient Israelitic, its functions, 25, 87; abolished by Deuteronomy, 85.

Paganism, in Israel and Judah, 38, 52, 74-75.
Palestine, 16, 26, 30.
Palestrina, his musical setting of the verses of Micah, 75.
Pantheon, of the heathen Semites, 21.
Passover, feast of, 23, 26.
Pastoral care of souls, 119 et seq.
Patriarchs, 72.
Pekah, king of Israel, attacks Ahaz of Judah, 62; conquered and executed by Tiglath-Pileser, 63.
Pentateuch, its analysis by De Wette, 83; juridical parts of the first books of, written by the post-exilic Babylonian Jews, 159.
Pentecost, the feast of, 86.
Pergamon, the kingdom of, 175.
Persecution, only intensifies religious zeal, 93.
Persians, under Cyrus, 129; their religion, 145; overthrow Babylon, 144, 156, and succor the Jews, 147; subdue Egypt, 149; consolidated by Darius, 150-154; their empire destroyed by Alexander the Great, 165.
Pharaoh, Egyptian king, 10.
Pharisaism, Judaism transformed into, 176.
Philistines, 43, 44.
Phœnician prophets, 12.
Phraortes, king of the Medes, lays siege to Nineveh, 77.
Pindar, 11.
Plat, I will requite thee in this, 32.
Ploughshares, turned into swords, 165.
Polytheism, 24.
Potter, as the, treadeth clay, 134.

Pouring out of the spirit, 165.
Praise, shall call thy gates, 140.
Prayer, my house a house of, 140.
Precious from the vile, freeing the, 94, 171.
Prepare ye in the wilderness a way, 132.
Priesthood, old Israelitic conception of, modified by Deuteronomy, 87 et seq.; all its members descended from the tribe of Levi, 87; gradually takes the place of prophecy, 90; its transformation in the post-exilic period, 149; its postexilic backsliding from God, 156.
Priestly code, of the post-exilic Babylonian Jews, also called the fundamental writing of the Pentateuch, 159-160.
Prince of the New Jerusalem, in Ezekiel, 122-124.
Prophecy, compared to a sealed book, 1; pre-requisites of a knowledge of, 2; meaning of the term, 3-15; originally a foreign element in the Israelitic religion, 14; its activity always coincident with historical catastrophes, 34-35; the rise of written, 37 et seq.; its practical influence in Isaiah, 68; attacks the religion of the people, 71; how influenced by Deuteronomy, 82 et seq.; abdicates in favor of the priesthood, 89-90; Jeremiah's conception of, 93-94, 95; reaches its highest consummation in Jeremiah, 98; wins a triumph over the popular religion in the Babylonian exile, 111; applied in the historical literature of Israel, 127; its character, etc., in the period after the exile, 149 et seq.; change of its style, in Zechariah, becoming literary in form, 152; lowest degradation and caricature of, in Zechariah, Chapters 9-14, 167-169; flares upward victorious for the last time in Jonah and Daniel, 169, 170, 177; Israel's costliest and noblest bequest to the world, 173, 179; superior to any other intellectual production of

mankind, 178; its relation to Christianity, 178; its tremendous significance to the world, 178; called Mary the mother of Christianity, 178; God's noblest gift of grace, 178.

Prophet, originally not a foreteller of the future, 5 et seq.; etymological analysis of the Hebrew word, 8-13; the primitive Canaanite type, 13 et seq.; the storm-petrels of the world's history, 35; the true character of the Israelitic prophet, 35 et seq.; Israel God's prophet to the whole earth, 141 et seq., 162.

προφήτης, Greek for prophet, meaning of, 5, 11.

Prophetic exposition of the history of Israel in the Babylonian exile, 126-128.

Prophets, general ignorance of their significance, 1-2; the schools of, 14 et seq., 28; the reaction against, under Manasseh, 71-79; their persecution infuses in them new life, 80; their influence with Josiah, 81; their altered relation to God after the exile, 152; the distinctive note of all their religious activity, 154; post-exilic reaction against their predictions, 155-156.

Pruning-hooks, turned into spears, 165.

Psaltery, tablet, etc., prophets with a, 12.

Ptolemies, the Egyptian, support the Jews, 175.

Pyrrhic victory of prophecy, 89.

Quietness, in, shall ye be saved, 57.

Ramah, place of worship, 26.
Razor, that is hired, shaved with, 63.
Rechabites, abstainers from wine, Jeremiah's approval of, 97.
Reed, a bruised, shall he not break, 142.
Reform, of Ezra and Nehemiah, 160 et seq.; of Josiah, 83, 90, 127.
Reins, God tries the heart and the, an expression coined by Jeremiah, 97.

Religion, Israel's first impulses always spring from, 27; as defined by Amos, 42; by Hosea, 52; saved by Isaiah, 69; its power among primitive peoples, 71, 108-109; its fundamental problem, the relation of God and the world, 83; Deuteronomy's conception of, 83-84, 89; Jeremiah's conception of, 96-99; Jesus's conception of, 84; reduced by Deuteronomy to three great feasts, 86-87; reaches its highest Old Testament consummation in Jeremiah, 98-99; Ezekiel's view of, 119; made a matter of a book by Deuteronomy, 152; its neglect after the exile, 157; universal, the idea of, first clearly conceived by Israelitic prophecy, 45, 178.

Remembrance-book, God's, 158.
Remnant, Isaiah's, 58, 63; sifted out in the Babylonian captivity, 113.
Rend, the kingdom out of the hand of Solomon, Behold I will, 28.
Resurrection of the dead, first taught as a postulate of faith in Isaiah, Chapters 24-27, 166-167; becomes a dogma in Daniel, 174.
Revealed religion, conception of, introduced by Deuteronomy, 90.
Revelry, at the ancient Israelitic festivals, 28 et seq.
Rezin, last king of Damascus, conquered and executed by Tiglath-Pileser, 62, 63.
Righteousness, in, shalt thou be established, 140; also 144, 166.
Robber, Assyrian compared to, 78.
Rock, beside Me, Is there a, 139.

Sabbath, known to the old Babylonians, 26; made a fundamental institution of Judaism by Ezekiel, 120-121.
Sacrifices, in ancient Israel, 37 et seq.; the ancient Israelitic conception of, 85-86; revolutionised by Deuteronomy, 87-88.

Salvation, by works, 159; thy walls, called, 140.
Samaria, 30, 39, 44, 118.
Samuel, not a prophet but a seer, 12; his character and historical import, 27-28; the mother of, at the festival of Shiloh, 38, 126.
Sanctuaries, the ancient local, 85.
Sanskrit, 9.
Sargon, Assyrian king, 64.
Saul, among the prophets, 12-13; his character misjudged, 28, 29.
Scales, weigh the mountains in, 136.
Scythians, devastate Asia, 76, 99.
Sealed book, prophecy a, 1.
Seamen, heathen, their behavior contrasted with that of Jonah's, 171.
Seed, holy, of Isaiah, 58.
Seer, for prophet, 12.
Seleucidæ, conquer Egypt and attempt to Hellenise the Jews, 176; repulsed by the Maccabees, 176-177.
Semites, their religion, 7; their language, 5 et seq.
Sennacherib, Assyrian king, 66; attacks Judah and besieges Jerusalem, 62, 72.
Seraiah, the last priest of the old temple of Jerusalem, 148.
Seraphs, original meaning of, 21.
Servant, Israel, my, 141-142.
Shake the heaven and the earth, 151.
Shaphan, Josiah's scribe, delivers Deuteronomy to the king, 81.
Sheep, like, for the slaughter, 94.
Shepherd, the Messiah compared to a good, by Ezekiel, 119; of God, Cyrus called the, 135.
Sheshbazzar, Persian commissary, heads the return of the Jews, 147.
Shiloh, place of worship, 26, 38.
Sichem, place of worship, 26;
Sieve, Babylonian captivity compared to a, 111.
Sign, from God, Ahaz challenged by Isaiah to ask for a, 62; between God and Israel, 121.
Signet, make Zerubbabel, as a, 151.
Sin, the propitiation of, as viewed by Deuteronomy, 88.
Sinai, its connexion with Moses and the religion of Israel, 18-21; peninsula of, 21.
Sins, Israel knew only sins, no crimes, 25; of Israel, the prophets' constant reference to, 164.
Sisera, the stars fight, 27.
Sistine Chapel, 75.
Slave, I am thy son and, 63.
Slaves, Hebrew, set free to save Jerusalem, but afterwards basely forced into new servitude, 105.
Slow of speech and tongue, 10.
Smith, makes idols, 137.
Sodom, justified, 118.
Solomon, his worship of idols, 23, 30; his despotic government, 23; interpretation of his supposed idolatry, 30; opens Israel to the world, 30.
Son of Man, expression used by Ezekiel, 116; designation of the Messianic ruler as the, in Daniel, 174.
Souls, Ezekiel's pastoral care of, 119 et seq.
Sour grapes, our fathers have eaten, etc., 117.
Spinoza, his view of the historical books of the Old Testament, 125.
Spirit, of wisdom and understanding, 60; the pouring out of the. 165.
Stars, Assyrian worship of, in Judæa, 74, 81, 118, 127; fight for Israel, 27.
State and Church, opposition of, created by Deuteronomy, 88-89, 114.
State, ecclesiastical, Ezekiel's ideal of, 122-124.
Strength, his God, 79.
Stubble, as driven, to his bow, 134.
Sycomore-fruit, gatherer of, 14, 41.
Symbols, in Zechariah's visions, 152.
Synagogue, excludes Daniel from the prophetic writings, 174.
Syncretism, religious, 31.
Syria, invaded by the Assyrians, 73; under Antiochus IV., 176.
Syrians, Have I not brought up the, from Kir, 43.

Tabernacles, feast of, 26, 86.
Tarshish (Tartessus), Jonah flees to, 171, 172.
Tatnai, Persian satrap, 154.

INDEX. 193

Tears, that my eyes were a fountain of, 95.
Teeth, prophets that bite with their, 35; children's on edge, 117.
Teiresias, soothsayer, 5.
Tekoa, Amos's home, 40.
Temple, the new, begun and completed, 151, 154; feeling of the Jews towards, 155.
Testify against me, 75.
Testimony, bind up the, 63.
Theocracy, so-called, of the Old Testament, originates with Hosea, 54; its realisation possible only under foreign rule, 123-124.
Theodicy, or vindication of God, the Jews' need of, in the exile, 125. See also *Ezekiel*.
Theology of history, Deutero-Isaiah's, 143.
Tiglath-Pileser, Assyrian king, the suzerain of Ahaz, conquers Damascus and Israel, 62-63.
Trumpet, Shall a, be blown? 35.
Tyre, 30.

Unchastity, religious, 23-24.
Unclean things in Assyria, eat, 109.
Universal, history, Isaiah's conception of, 57-58; religion, the idea of, first clearly conceived by Israelitic prophecy, 45, 178.
Urijah, prophet, executed by Jehoiakim, 100.
Uzziah, king, 61.

Vile, freeing of the precious from, 94, 171.
Vineyard of Naboth, 31 et seq.
Virgin, of Israel, is fallen, 40.
Visions, of Zechariah, 152-153.

Walther von der Vogelweide, 126.
Watchman, over the house of Israel, Ezekiel's definition of a prophet, 119; also 35.
Waters, O that my head were, 95.
Wearied, ye have, the Lord, 157.
Weeks, feast of, 26, 86.
Whale, Jonah's, 170.

Wickedness, wicked man, etc., 32, 119, 157, 158, 166.
Wine and strong drink, I will, prophesy of, 35.
Wine-drinking, Jeremiah on, 97.
Works, salvation by, in later Judaism, origin and meaning, 159.
Worm, Jacob as a, 112, 141.
Wormwood, justice turned to, 44.
Worship, paganism in, causes the decay of Israel, 71; the reforms of, by Hezekiah, 68; how viewed by the Jews, 72; by Josiah, 82, 83, 90; centralised by Deuteronomy in Jerusalem, 84-88.
Wrath, O day of, 76-77; cup of, 94, 101.
Writ, holy, idea of, introduced by Deuteronomy, 90.

Yahveh, original Hebrew pronunciation of Jehovah, 17; the name introduced by Moses, 18-19; etymological meaning, 19-21; originally a tempest-god worshipped on Mt. Sinai, 20-21; worshipped under the image of a bull, 37, 52; His exclusiveness and intimate relation to Israel, 25, 31; prophets of, 30.
Yokes of wood, thou hast broken, etc., 103.

Zarephath, the widow of, succored by Elijah, 31.
Zebaoth, the Lord of Hosts, a name coined by Amos, 46.
Zeboim, Shall I set thee as, 52.
Zechariah, prophet, 152-153; vision of, 2.
Zechariah, Chapters 9-14, dates from the third century, shows the lowest degradation of the prophetic literature of Israel, 167-169.
Zedekiah, king of Judah, seated on the throne by Nebuchadnezzar, 1-2; his revolt against Nebuchadnezzar, 103-104; taken captive and led to Babylon in chains, 105-106.
Zephaniah, prophet, 76 et seq.; his description of Josiah's corrupt court, 81.

Zerubbabel, grandson of king Jehoiachin, minister of Sheshbazzar, 148; Persian viceroy of Judæa, hailed as the Messianic King by Haggai, 150-151, and by Zechariah, 152; receives the golden crown from the Jews of Babylon, 154; lays the foundations of the second temple, 151, and completes it, 154.

Zeus, 11.

Zion, Isaiah's dogma of the inviolability of, 65, 75, 103-104; the opposed doctrine in Micah, 70; the dwelling-place of God, 84; the feast of the converted nations on, 166.

www.ingramcontent.com/pod-product-compliance
Lightning Source LLC
Chambersburg PA
CBHW020859230426
43666CB00008B/1242